Confronting Marginalisation in Education

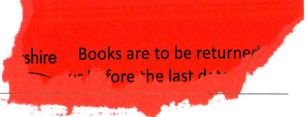

One of the key challenges facing schools today is that of reducing marginalisation amongst pupils in educational contexts. This timely book provides guidance and illustrative examples of the ways in which primary and secondary schools can include all of their students in the academic and social experiences they provide. Developed around a framework that practitioners and researchers can use in order to understand and address marginalisation, the author's approach takes account of the views of children and young people throughout. This framework consists of a unique four-step process:

- **Step 1:** Opening doors: enabling voices to emerge
- **Step 2:** Looking closely: bringing concerns to the surface
- **Step 3:** Making sense of the evidence: sharing data with learners
- **Step 4:** Dealing with marginalisation: encouraging inclusive thinking and practice.

By helping practitioners to reach out to all learners, regardless of the labels assigned to them, the book explains how teachers can make sure that every child matters, and, in so doing, create a classroom that is all the more inclusive. Importantly, the book focuses on *all* learners, including those who might experience marginalisation but whose voices might have not previously been heard.

Relevant to teachers of pupils of all ages, students on initial teacher education, and undergraduate and postgraduate students, this book will also be of interest to researchers and academics who are focusing on the role of children's voices in promoting inclusive education.

Kyriaki Messiou is Senior Lecturer at the University of Hull, UK.

Confronting Marginalisation in Education

A framework for promoting inclusion

Kyriaki Messiou

Routledge
Taylor & Francis Group

LONDON AND NEW YORK

First published 2012
by Routledge
2 Park Square, Milton Park, Abingdon, Oxon OX14 4RN

Simultaneously published in the USA and Canada
by Routledge
711 Third Avenue, New York, NY 10017
Routledge is an imprint of the Taylor & Francis Group, an informa business

British Library Cataloguing in Publication Data
A catalogue record for this book is available from the British Library

Library of Congress Cataloging in Publication Data
Messiou, Kyriaki.
Confronting marginalisation in education : a framework for promoting inclusion / Kyriaki Messiou.
p. cm.
1. Children with social disabilities—Education. 2. Children with social disabilities—Education (Primary) 3. Inclusive education. 4. Marginality, Social .
I. Title.
LC4065.M47 2012
371.826'94–dc23
2011044186

ISBN: 978–0–415–60350–8 (hbk)
ISBN: 978–0–415–60351–5 (pbk)
ISBN: 978–0–203–12118–4 (ebk)

Typeset in Bembo by Prepress Projects, Ltd, Perth, UK

Printed and bound in Great Britain by
TJ International Ltd, Padstow, Cornwall

To those children and young people whose voices may never be heard

Contents

Figures

Preface

This, my first book, is a result of a long-term engagement in the field of education, wearing different hats at different times: practitioner, researcher, academic, co-researcher. Many times people have asked me why marginalisation, where does this interest come from? It is not easy to answer this, but I guess working in schools for a long time, observing the kind of unfairness that sometimes surrounds particular students, led me to develop a particular interest in wanting to find out more – and, more importantly, to do something about it. In essence, this is what this book attempts to do.

A number of people have been influential for my work throughout the years: those who have helped me in refining my thinking, those who allowed me the space and freedom to make my dreams a reality, and those who showed me that there is a possibility for change. These are the people I would like to thank here.

First of all, I wish to acknowledge the contributions of all those children whom I taught, or worked with as a researcher. They taught me a great deal. They surprised me, they confronted me, they made me stop and think and, in so doing, pushed my thinking forward. Second, in my most recent role as a university lecturer, thanks go to my students, both undergraduate and postgraduate, who took on similar roles: challenging me, as well as supporting and embracing my ideas.

A headteacher I was fortunate enough to work with back in Cyprus, Mrs Popi Loizidou, has to be thanked here too: for believing in me and supporting my work, as well as giving me the space to operate in a rather tight system; and for being such an inspirational leader.

The other headteacher who has been, and continues to be, a true inspiration for me is my sister, Dr Demetra Messiou. She has been a leading example for many school teachers in Cyprus and observing her work has taught me a great deal. The discussions we had throughout all these years have shaped my thinking and practices in many ways. Special thanks on reading and commenting on earlier drafts of this book.

In 1995, as a postgraduate student, I attended the inaugural lecture of Professor Mel Ainscow at the University of Manchester. He was the newly appointed professor. There were several announcements inviting us to attend the lecture. It was the title of the lecture that drew my attention: 'Effective schools for all'. That lecture, which inspired me and in a way reassured me that there are others who hold similar beliefs to mine, provided me with the evidence that when there is a will there is a way. The lecture was life-changing for me, as was working with Mel subsequently.

The completion of this book would have not been possible without the support from my own institution and my colleagues at the University of Hull. Hull has opened up doors to me and I will always be grateful for this.

Last but not least, my parents, Marina and Stavros, who, having nothing to do with education as a discipline, had everything to do with my own education. I owe everything to them.

Thanks to all of you.

Kyriaki Messiou
Hull
August 2011

Introduction
Bus journeys

Some people complain about using public transport; others seem to enjoy it. For me, the bus simply provides a very convenient and cost-effective way to get to work. At the same time, it has ended up being a very enjoyable way, as well as sometimes being thought-provoking.

Many days I end up getting the bus at the same time that children are going to school. Less often, as I usually finish work later, I end up getting the bus back home when they are on their way back from school. These times, I have to admit, tend to be less enjoyable. Interestingly enough, the students at that time are usually far happier and talkative – in fact, loud at times – and I would like to think that this is because they are awake by that time, contrary to the morning. Or they might even be happier that school has finished for the day!

What both kinds of journey provide me with are opportunities to think further about the importance of engaging with students' voices. I consider myself to be a natural observer, and in this case I try intentionally to listen to what students say. Some would argue that this is not ethically right and, of course, in England, it might well be perceived as being rude. On the other hand, I do not think that any of the students that I listen to are trying in any way not to be heard. What I listen to is heard by almost everyone on the bus and, anyway, the students will remain anonymous – as they are anonymous to me – even though some of their faces have become so familiar. I hope the students whose words I am going to use would not mind. In the end, what I am trying to do here is to help others think about the potential of engaging with students' voices.

Listening to children and young people

Bearing all of this in mind, in what follows I describe four incidents from my bus journeys. At the end of each account, I raise some questions for reflection.

Incident 1

> A secondary school student gets on the bus. Half asleep, half awake, he sits in front of me. At the next bus stop a secondary school girl comes on and sits next to him. They start chatting. The boy looks sad. The girl asks him if everything is OK. He starts telling her how his father beat his mother up again this morning and kicked her out of the house, and how upset he is about it. He asks the girl to promise that she will not say anything to anyone, that this will be their secret, and she agrees to that. She also tries to reassure him that things will get better ...

Reflective questions

I wonder what happened when the boy got to school. He asked his friend to keep a secret, signalling to me that he had no intention of sharing this information with any of the adults in the school. Is it possible that this boy was in a position to pay attention to his teachers and engage with learning on that day? How would his teachers respond to him being absent minded? Would they approach him and ask him sensitively what was wrong? Would they shout at him? If they knew, would they have any expectations from that boy on that particular day? How many students might be going to school with similar 'baggage' every morning? Do teachers truly give students the opportunity to express themselves and reveal such issues that have a bearing on their learning? What more can practitioners do?

Incident 2

> A primary-age boy, white skinned, gets on the bus with his dad. They sit at the back of the bus. A boy of what appears to be African heritage gets on at the next stop, with his mother. He immediately sees the other boy and happily calls his name, 'Eddie' (not his real name), and runs towards him. The mother calls him to come to the front and sit with her. The boy does not listen to her and stays with his friend and the dad. The mum looks very worried and keeps looking towards the back. When they get off the bus she grasps his hand and starts whispering something in his ear.

Reflective questions

Isn't it lovely that the children from different ethnic backgrounds are so accepting of one another? I bet their teachers have done a great job in ensuring this building of relationships in a city which is predominantly white. How can we sustain this? How can we listen carefully to what these stories are telling us for promoting acceptance of diversity and inclusion of all – within schools and outside schools? What more can be done?

Incident 3

> It is the first week that the students are back at school. Two secondary school boys sit behind me. One of them takes outs his timetable and says 'Right, let's see what we have today. History . . . I hate it. English . . . I hate it . . . Maths . . . I hate it . . .' and so on. His friend is laughing.

Reflective questions

I want to ask: Why? What is it that you hate? I am very well aware of how teenagers behave and talk these days. But I am worried. Maybe it is me, maybe I am too romantic, or maybe I take everything very seriously, but I would want to know. I wonder how many students have similar feelings; not necessarily using the same strong words but being bored with learning and school, disengaged and uninterested? And, more importantly, what more can be done to change this situation?

Incident 4

> A group of Polish girls are chatting, sometimes in English and occasionally in their own language. They are very loud and laughing all the time. Another group of English girls are standing close to them. All the girls go to the same school. The English girls are looking at them and one of them starts making nasty remarks – for me, it was definitely verbal bullying. The Polish girls start answering in their own language. At the end of each word or sentence, all the Polish girls are laughing. The English girls look puzzled, not knowing how to react. At the next stop the English girls get off the bus. As they walk along by the bus they make facial expressions and rude gestures to the Polish girls.

Reflective questions

Who is marginalising whom in this example? It seems that the use of the Polish language was a way that these girls could respond to the verbal bullying directed at them. How much of this is going on in their schools? To what extent are teachers aware of it? What is happening in schools in order to address this issue? I do not doubt that practitioners are trying to address such issues in schools but, if as soon as they leave the school gates the students behave like this, then certainly it seems to me that there is more that needs to be done.

This book aims to address the recurring question that emerges in relation to each of these accounts: *what more can be done in schools?* The way that this is achieved is through the use of a framework which facilitates a research process that focuses on an engagement with students' voices in schools in order to confront marginalisation and promote inclusion.

Why marginalisation?

My interest in marginalisation emerged over a number of years. Having being a mainstream primary school teacher for over fifteen years, I came to see how certain individuals within schools become marginalised in a variety of ways. Sometimes the marginalisation I witnessed was in relation to academic factors, whereas on other occasions it had to do with social relationships, or, indeed, it related to both. Many times, factors that seemed to create marginalisation were obvious, although at other times they were not.

I will never forget one student of mine in Year 6, who was really struggling with learning in all respects, despite the fact that he was trying very hard. Each classroom had a library from which students could borrow books to take home and read. The students had to fill in their own cards showing what they took out and when, and equally when they brought the books back. We had also introduced a rewards system whereby the student who read most books at the end of each month received a certificate. To my surprise, I saw how this boy's book list was getting longer and longer. One day, I noticed him take a book that was at Year 6 level – which I knew he could not read – and, at the same time, in this book he hid another very easy one so that nobody could see. I did not say anything to him but the incident made me realise how he must have felt and what this had led him to do. At the same time, it made me realise how our own actions as teachers can push some students towards the margins.

This interest led me to want to work with students perceived as the most marginalised within school contexts: those defined as having special educational needs. This, in turn, led me to undertake postgraduate studies in England in relation to this specialism, only to realise that the ways in which support was offered for this group of learners – most times outside the mainstream class – was in itself a way of setting them apart from others.

It was during that period that I came across the concept of inclusive education, an idea that opened up new horizons. Specifically, I began to see how inclusive education was about respecting diversity of learners, and finding ways to address contextual barriers to learning and participation within schools (Booth and Ainscow, 2002). It seemed to me that inclusive education could be the way to address marginalisation in schools. At the same time, I could see how the introduction of such thinking into schools would be challenging and, sometimes, turbulent.

As I continued on to my doctoral studies I became particularly interested in the role of students' voices in relation to the development of more inclusive forms of education. This led me to study, in detail, how marginalisation is perceived by children of primary school age. The research I carried out at that time led me to argue that marginalisation in schools is far from straightforward and can be conceptualised in a number of ways.

Becoming a lecturer at the University of Hull enabled me to carry out further research around these themes, in various school contexts. The more schools that I visited the more I could see how issues related to marginalisation exist, many times in subtle forms. I also saw how teachers struggle to address such issues. This book is based on all of these experiences, all of which involved research that aimed to make a difference to schools, as well as to the experiences of individual students.

Research that makes a difference

This book addresses the question: *how can schools engage with students' voices in order to confront marginalisation and promote inclusion?* More specifically, it sets out to help schools – and researchers working with them – explore different ways in which marginalisation is experienced by children and young people in order that it can be confronted. In this way, I aim to help teachers 'reach out to all learners', regardless of the labels that are assigned to them, making sure that every child matters, and, in so doing, making their classrooms more inclusive.

At the same time, the book will be of relevance to researchers that are interested in research that makes a difference and that has a direct impact on the lives of people in schools. This orientation, in which researchers work as 'outsiders' alongside participants in schools, is intended to overcome the traditional gap between research and practice (Ainscow *et al.*, 2006).

The approach I describe has been developed as a result of extensive research in schools over a period of ten years or so, all of which has had a particular focus on marginalisation. The examples I use come from school contexts in England and Cyprus, my home country, where I worked in the past. Using examples from both countries indicates the potential to use the approach I am recommending in different contexts.

The specific focus is on the use of the voices of students in schools to reveal those who are most likely to experience some kind of marginalisation, as well as issues that are related to the inclusion of all. The text is developed around a framework that can be used in order to understand and, more importantly, address marginalisation. This framework encourages an engagement with students' voices in schools in a more meaningful way. In this way, I intend that adults working in schools will become more sensitive to the potential of listening to what children and young people have to say.

Overview of the chapters

The book is organised in seven chapters in addition to the introduction and the conclusion. Chapter 1 explores the concept of marginalisation in education. In order to do this it examines the ways in which marginalisation has been defined in the research literature, as well as looking at the issue of labelling (particularly the use of the term 'special educational needs') and the links with marginalisation. It is argued that labelling does not necessarily lead to students being overlooked. At the same time, it explains how, by focusing only on labels, we might be overlooking some learners who are truly experiencing marginalisation. Then four ways of conceptualising marginalisation are presented, as these emerged from my earlier work. This is followed by a discussion around how engaging with students' voices can lead to better understandings of marginalisation. Links between marginalisation and inclusion are also made. Towards the end of the chapter the framework for understanding and dealing with marginalisation is introduced. This involves four steps, each of which is explained in the subsequent chapters.

Chapter 2 presents an example from a school where the framework was used by practitioners with minimum input from me as a researcher. This account demonstrates the impact that this had on individuals and on the school as a whole. Towards the end of the chapter, some areas that need to be considered before getting started with the framework are discussed, including ethical considerations that relate to engaging with students' voices.

In Chapter 3, the first step of the framework, 'Opening doors: enabling voices to emerge', is described. Specifically, a range of practical approaches for identifying marginalisation are described. Ethical issues related to the use of these approaches with children about such sensitive issues is discussed. The main focus is on different methods and techniques that can be used in order to bring to the surface the views of pupils. Illustrative examples of the use of these techniques are provided.

Chapter 4 analyses the second step of the framework, 'Looking closely: bringing concerns to the surface'. It discusses the importance of stopping to think about the reactions of pupils to the experiences they have in school. Ideas of how to single out data and information that might be of concern are discussed, as well as how to decide what information to share with students and staff in the next step. Consideration is given to how this analysis can be used as part of ongoing school development processes, so as to benefit both students and practitioners who work in very busy contexts. The importance of involving colleagues and others as critical friends in this process is discussed.

In Chapter 5, the third step of the framework, 'Making sense of the evidence: sharing data with learners', is described. Here, strategies for sharing data and information with pupils and other staff members are explored. It should be noted here that the term 'learners' is used in relation to everybody taking part in this step. In this way, it is emphasised that in this process all take the role of learners. In other words, through the process all engage in meaningful conversations with one another, and, therefore, learn from one another. It is stressed that this sharing of information is not a straightforward process, and that it can sometimes lead to fruitful tensions in bringing to the surface issues that are difficult to discuss and deal with. This is, without doubt, the most crucial step in the whole process, which, if dealt with carefully, usually lead to the next step, that of confronting marginalisation.

Chapter 6 addresses ways of dealing with marginalisation. It follows on naturally from the previous step since, through the sharing of information, the seeds of changes in thinking are likely to be planted. However, it is viewed as a separate step since substantial changes in thinking, and more importantly practice, need time to take place. It is argued that in order to deal with marginalisation learners have to find ways to act on the issues that have emerged from the earlier steps in the process. Examples from schools contexts are once again used to illustrate how engaging with students' voices had an impact on the thinking of individuals, as well as on the practices used. The main argument in this chapter is that in order to deal with marginalisation we must develop this form of collaborative, evidence-based thinking and acting within particular contexts, and that this can be achieved through the use of the four-step process.

Chapter 7 presents a discussion around the whole process of the framework as a way of addressing marginalisation. Particular attention is paid to the importance of seeing the framework as a cyclical process that has to become a continual and never-ending aspect of the work and culture of a school. This further emphasises the importance of seeing marginalisation as a complex, multi-faceted notion and the process of dealing with it as being equally, if not more, complex. In addition, a refined version of the framework is presented. Finally, the chapter argues that an engagement with students' voices represents a distinctive approach to inclusive education.

The book concludes with a short reflection on the implications of the arguments presented in the previous chapters.

Chapter 1

Conceptualising marginalisation

This chapter explores the concept of marginalisation in education, as well as how the concept relates to inclusion. In order to do this it considers the ways in which marginalisation has been defined in the literature, as well as looking at the issue of labelling (particularly the use of the term 'special educational needs') and the links with marginalisation. It is argued that labelling does not necessarily lead to pupils being overlooked. At the same time, it explains how, by focusing only on those students who are defined as being in some sense vulnerable, we might be overlooking others who are experiencing marginalisation.

Drawing on my own research, marginalisation is defined as taking one of four forms: (i) when a child is experiencing some kind of marginalisation that is recognised almost by everybody, including himself/herself; (ii) when a child is feeling that he/she is experiencing marginalisation, whereas most of the others do not recognise this; (iii) when a child is found in what appears to be marginalised situations but does not feel it, or does not view it as marginalisation; and, finally, (iv) when a child is experiencing marginalisation but does not admit it. This means that marginalisation must be regarded as a complex, multi-faceted notion that has to be explored in relation to specific contexts.

An exploration of the importance of engaging with students' voices follows, since the potential of engaging with their views is central to the rationale on which the framework recommended in this book was developed. In addition to this, the rationale on which the framework is based is described. This places a particular focus on the links between marginalisation and the notion of inclusion as a concept that relates to different ways in which schools can respond to the diversity of their learners. Towards the end of the chapter the suggested framework for understanding and confronting marginalisation is introduced, before subsequent chapters go into details of each individual step.

Marginalisation in education

Marginalisation is an abstract and complex concept. It has been used in various disciplines, such as psychology, sociology and most recently education. UNESCO's Education for All (EFA) Global Monitoring Report (UNESCO,

2010), entitled *Reaching the Marginalized*, argues that in all countries, regardless whether rich or poor, there are individuals and groups that experience extreme and persistent disadvantage in education, which as a consequence sets them apart from society. It is also argued in the report that, although defining marginalisation is difficult, most people would accept that it encompasses quantitative deprivation, as measured by years in school or the level of education attained. In addition, it is noted that there is a qualitative dimension of marginalisation: those who are defined as marginalised typically demonstrate lower levels of educational achievement.

Using UNESCO's dimensions of quantitative versus qualitative, it can be argued that lack of access to education is the ultimate form of marginalisation in education, or to be more accurate marginalisation from education. In other words, the 67 million children out of school globally in 2009 (UIS, 2011) are without doubt the ones who are most marginalised. However, that is not the focus of this book. Rather, the focus here is on more subtle forms of marginalisation that exist once children and young people are in schools. In other words, the concern here is with marginalisation within school contexts.

The concept of marginalisation can be found in the theory of the 'marginal man', which initially emphasised the specific personality traits that individuals develop when placed in a marginal situation between two not entirely compatible social positions (Dickie-Clark, 1966). However, as the theory evolved, more emphasis was placed upon the sociological perspective of the marginal situation and how it specifically affected the structure and functioning of groups. Dickie-Clark points out that 'the very notion of "marginal" suggests limits or boundaries of some kinds as well as the juxtaposition of entities' (p. 28). Following this definition, one might argue that a common practice used in schools in many countries – that of separating individuals from their peers in order to provide additional support – can be described as a kind of setting limits or boundaries. Since it certainly involves one kind of boundary, it can be described as a form of marginalisation. However, what is absent from this argument is the experience and perceptions of the people involved in the process. For example, even though such situations might be described as 'marginalising' by others, they might not be experienced as such by those involved, as research suggests (e.g. Belanger, 2000; Messiou, 2003). Therefore, I argue that what counts as marginalisation involves subjective interpretations. Consequently, it is essential to engage with the views of those who are found in such situations.

Similar thinking relates to the idea of labelling. 'Labelling theory' is a term associated with Howard Becker (1973), whose work focused on deviance. He suggests that all social groups make rules and attempt, at some time and under some circumstances, to enforce them. According to Becker, those who break these rules are regarded as 'outsiders'. However, sometimes those defined by others as outsiders might themselves perceive others as outsiders, since they do not agree with the rules that are imposed upon them. For Becker, 'The deviant is one to whom that label has successfully been applied; deviant behaviour is behaviour that people so label' (p. 9). If we extend this thinking to marginalisation, we could argue that marginal behaviour is what people have labelled as such. In other words, those who are perceived by others as deviating from what is perceived to be the 'norm' could be given the label of marginal. This could also have an impact on the way that others are behaving towards those whom they have labelled as marginal.

Becker's ideas are compatible, to some extent, with the premises of symbolic interactionism. Adopting this perspective, Blumer (1969) argues that human beings act towards things on the basis of the meanings they have for them, and those meanings arise out of the social interaction between people and are then modified through an interpretative process that is used by the person in dealing with the things he/she encounters. Therefore, emphasis is placed on the meanings held by people concerning others, or even labels that are assigned to people, and the way in which meanings are created. Following Becker's ideas, and using notions of symbolic interactionism, I take the position that marginalisation is created in social groups, and through the interactions and labelling that occur within them (Messiou, 2006a).

In a way that relates to these ideas, the UNDP (1996) defines marginalisation as 'the state of being considered unimportant, undesirable, unworthy, insignificant and different resulting in inequity, unfairness, deprivation and enforced lack of access to mainstream power' (p. 1). This definition suggests that if individuals are considered, either by others or by themselves, as unimportant or undesirable, they are experiencing marginalisation, with all the potential consequences I have described.

Taking Dickie-Clark's definition of marginalisation – with its particular focus on limits or boundaries of various kinds, and the juxtaposition of individuals – it becomes evident that processes of marginalisation are closely linked to labelling. So, by defining a child as 'having special educational needs', for example, we are juxtaposing individuals, and, therefore, it is possible that some individuals come to be marginalised. Similarly, this same argument could extend to other groups of learners, such as children from different ethnic backgrounds, travellers and those in public care. In saying that, it must be noted that simply belonging to one of these groups does not necessarily mean that individuals will experience marginalisation. What it does mean, though, is that, most of the time, belonging in those groups attaches labels to those individuals. Usually, these labels do not hold a positive connotation in education contexts; rather, students who are assigned labels are often seen as learners who present potential challenges for school contexts.

The issue of labelling

My own engagement with children as a practitioner for many years – as well as my engagement in the field as a researcher – has led me to doubt the necessity of thinking about students as belonging to distinct groups and, even more dangerously, labelling them. As a practitioner, I am aware of the fact that this is sometimes seen to be helpful, since, for example, bilingual students might well face similar difficulties in schools. Responses that have helped a particular student might, therefore, prove to be helpful with another child belonging to the same group. Some would argue that this applies particularly to those learners defined as having special educational needs. However, one has to keep in mind that, although a child might fall into one group, at the same time he/she falls into other categories, such as boys and girls or nine-year-olds, for example, and, most importantly, they are each individuals with different personalities, interests, strengths and weaknesses that one has to take into account when working with them. Therefore, rather than making assumptions based on which group a learner belongs to, I feel that a much more useful approach is that of engaging with each student as an individual.

In addition, and most importantly, focusing only on labels can be very limiting in that it deflects attention from wider contextual factors that bear on a student's learning and participation (Ainscow, 2000). This emphasis on contextual factors relates to the notion of inclusion and how this is understood in this book, a theme that I return to in a later section of this chapter.

Such arguments lead one to look critically at the stacks of books that are available that provide recipes to follow – especially regarding students defined as having a special educational need or a disability – suggesting that what works with one particular child works with others who fall into that group. It has to be acknowledged that some of the techniques suggested in these books can be quite useful; that is why they are so popular, especially among busy practitioners. The point that I am making is that such techniques in themselves can never be enough. Rather, the use of specific techniques has to be embedded within an approach that looks at individuals and tries to engage them to the greatest possible extent in the learning processes, as well as looking at factors within a given context that might create barriers to their participation and learning; whereas the suggestions made in some texts are, I feel, misleading in the way that they present complex challenges – such as meeting the needs of individual students – as straightforward issues that can be addressed by simply following a series of steps. At the same time, there is the danger of practitioners believing that they have done enough, since they have exhausted the formulaic approaches that are suggested. Therefore, sometimes, when the suggestions are not working they feel that there is nothing more that they can do, since they have already tried everything suggested in the books. This, I feel, prevents them from being creative and innovative in addressing challenges they are facing with particular learners.

A further concern I have is that a reliance on labels can lead to assumptions that students who fall in a particular group are necessarily experiencing marginalisation. This, in turn, may lead to specific ways of treating individuals. This reminds me of a recent example at my university. In my role as disability tutor, a student who had been diagnosed as having dyspraxia told me how her lecturer kept asking her in the class: 'Have you understood this? Let me explain it one more time.' Though the student was not complaining and appreciated her lecturer's efforts to help her, she said that she had no difficulties in understanding what they were taught and that there was, therefore, no need for her to be treated differently from any other student. It seemed to me that the fact that the student was assigned the particular label led her lecturer to assume that she could not understand and therefore needed further explanations.

Similarly, when I am working with practitioners in schools and I ask them to think about students who might be on the margins, often they immediately mention those who have been assigned some sort of a label. Alternatively, they may mention children who belong to particular groups that are assumed to be on the margins, such as those with disabilities, travellers, ethnic minorities, or people from low socio-economic backgrounds. I am not in any way blaming practitioners for thinking in such ways. In fact, I once had a similar response when I was talking to an academic about my own work. Her immediate response when I said that my work is about marginalisation was: 'Marginalisation of whom? For which group of learners?' It seems to me that this is the product of the dominant deficit thinking about individuals who belong in particular groups. For practitioners in England, this is the result of contradictory national policies. For example, I always thought it was very interesting that on the web-site of the Department for Children, Schools and Families – now renamed the Department for Education under the new government – there was an emphasis on inclusion for all, whilst, at the same time, material related to distinct categories of special educational needs, ethnic minorities, and gifted and talented also appeared as separate sections. This seems to suggest that, whereas inclusion is for all, at the same time we do know that there are some students who belong in particular groups that will experience marginalisation of some kind. Although learners falling in one of these categories might, in fact, experience marginalisation of some kind, in my view taking this for granted is dangerous. Most importantly, as I have explained, it can lead to overlooking others who experience marginalisation. Therefore, encouraging teachers to think in broader terms about all of this is necessary. From my experience in working with practitioners, when I encourage them to think further about initial responses of the sort that I have mentioned, they always come up with students whom they had never considered before. Often these are ones who get lost in the busy context of a school, where, understandably, attention is focused on those students perceived as being most vulnerable.

My argument here does not focus in any further detail on the use of labels in education, and the advantages and disadvantages involved. This has been discussed extensively in the literature (e.g. Lauchlan and Boyle, 2007) and could be a chapter in itself. The most overarching theme in favour of labelling is that of provision of additional resources in schools, which is certainly the case in the English context, whereas those who argue against labels discuss how they lead to stigmatising of individuals. These arguments, of course, might differ in other countries, as labelling does not automatically mean access to additional resources but might only have the damaging effects of stigmatising people.

However, this is not the focus of my own argument here. Rather, the central argument I am making is that labelling should *not* be seen as synonymous with marginalisation. As I have argued, there is a danger that, if seen as such, this might lead us to overlook the experiences of others who do not fall into any of the traditional groups. In a way that reinforces my argument, Veck (2009) suggests that 'labelling learners, in terms of what has been deemed deficient within them, can form a barrier to listening' (p. 142). So, for example, those defined as having a special educational need may not be given a chance to express their views on the assumption that they are not able to articulate them. In this way, perceptions of deficiency create a barrier to listening.

Although agreeing with this view, I argue that the absence of an assigned label can also lead to children not being listened to. As examples from research have shown (e.g. Derrington and Kendall, 2003; Lawson, 2010), a voice has been given to those individuals or groups of learners that fall into particular categories (for example, those defined as having special educational needs or travellers and gypsies). As a result, voices that were previously absent are now far more likely to be heard. On the other hand, accounts of the views of those who do not belong to particular groups – and who might also experience some kind of marginalisation in school contexts – are almost completely absent from the literature.

Understanding marginalisation

In trying to understand marginalisation, there is a need to move beyond a limited focus on particular groups assumed to be vulnerable, and this is certainly what I have attempted to do through my earlier work. This move presumes that marginalisation can have various meanings among different people and in different contexts. In particular, through my earlier doctoral work, I carried out an ethnographic study that set out to explore how marginalisation is experienced by children themselves in a primary school (Messiou, 2003). This led me to argue that marginalisation can be conceptualised in one of the four following ways:

1 when a child experiences some kind of marginalisation that is recognised by almost everybody including himself/herself
2 when a child feels that he/she is experiencing marginalisation whereas most of the others do not recognise this
3 when a child is found in what appear to be marginalised situations but does not feel it, or does not view it as marginalisation and, finally,
4 when a child is experiencing marginalisation but does not admit it.

The emergence of these four ways was influenced by the views of children themselves and the perceptions of teachers, as well as my observations within the particular context. Details about the methodology of the study, as well as examples from the fieldwork for each of the above ways with reference to particular children, can be found in articles that I have published earlier (e.g. Messiou, 2006a,b, 2008a). In what follows, I explain ways of conceptualising marginalisation in relation to four broad groupings that emerged from the study.

Group 1: The child experiences some kind of marginalisation that is recognised by almost everybody, including himself/herself

These children were the easiest to identify, since they were very open about their feelings. Their views were confirmed by others in the school and I was also in a position to observe their experiences of marginalisation. Children placed in this group talked very easily about their marginalisation. They were often outspoken, giving me examples from the year that I was carrying out the fieldwork and from previous years as well. Everybody knew, and they knew it and felt it as well. So children who belonged in this group explained clearly how they felt unhappy with certain situations they experienced.

Most children placed in this group were found to be actively making efforts to be included and to change situations, even though they were sometimes the ones experiencing the most severe forms of marginalisation. The fact that they were acknowledging that they were marginalised made them more outspoken about it, on the one hand, and act in more dynamic ways, on the other hand.

Group 2: The child feels that he/she is experiencing marginalisation whereas most of the others do not recognise this

Children included in this category were identified as such based mainly on the way that they felt. In these cases, therefore, there was not usually agreement among the three perspectives (children's, teachers', researcher's). The one perspective that was most taken into consideration was that of the child. My observations did not always agree with what these children were saying. In most cases, my view was that they were, in fact, experiencing occasional instances of rejection from other children. Similarly, their teachers' opinions mostly did not agree with the perceptions of these children. Nevertheless, what the children described to me was the way they felt. Hence, since they said they felt this way, I could not see any reason why I should not believe them. Whether the incidents they described really happened or not did not matter much, since it was these children's view of their reality. On what grounds could I decide that my perspective, or that of teachers, was more valid than these children's perceptions?

Children in this category were also very outspoken about their experiences, probably because they were feeling that most people did not believe them.

Therefore, it is likely they were trying to convince others that what they were feeling was the truth.

Group 3: The child is found in what appear to be marginalised situations but does not feel it, or does not view it as marginalisation

Children who belonged in this group were sometimes found in marginalised situations, for example, when receiving support separately from their peers, or not being accepted during playtime by others and being entirely on their own. However, they did not view those experiences as marginalisation and, in not viewing them as such, did not have any effect on their responses either. In other words, they seemed very relaxed and were not found to be making any efforts to change the situation. In a sense, they were just going with the flow of the situation. It has to be made clear here that most of the children who belonged in this group did not have any kind of communication difficulties that would prevent them from understanding what they were going through, or in expressing their views. There was, however, one girl defined as being on the autistic spectrum disorder who did experience some communication difficulties. In the case of this particular child, I could not be certain whether she did not see herself as being marginalised, or perhaps she could not explain this because of difficulties related to her ability to use language for the purpose of communication.

Of course, it is very difficult to really know whether these children truly did not view or feel that it was marginalisation that they were going through, or if rather they did not admit it. On reflection, I suppose that I put more emphasis on their behaviour, which suggested that they did not really see it as marginalisation. So children from this group behaved in a way that did not cause any concern within their school. Usually they joined others in their games and participated in any way they could. In the classrooms, they were doing whatever they could do and when they did not know what to do they either stopped working or might copy from their partners, without being anxious that they were not doing well.

Group 4: The child is experiencing marginalisation but does not admit it

The difference between this group of children and the previous one is that these children, through their words and actions, though never explicitly saying that they felt they were experiencing any kind of marginalisation, were in some sort of way saying that they knew what was happening. This could be either through what they were saying or doing, or through what they were not saying.

The fact that this group of children was not admitting their experiences of marginalisation suggested to me that they were trying to hide it from others and, perhaps, denying it to themselves. Their effort not to show anything and to cover what they were experiencing might indicate that deep down they were going through a lot of pain. In a way, it can be said that these children were masking their experiences as a way of dealing with them.

Concerning the four conceptualisations of marginalisation it has to be noted that these are not robust categories into which any student who is possibly experiencing marginalisation can be confidently put, but rather suggestions for thinking about marginalisation as experienced by students in relation to certain contexts.

The emergence of these four ways of thinking about marginalisation led me to redefine the concept. As I have described elsewhere (Messiou, 2006a), I consider the experience of inclusion to be akin to being inside a circle, and the experience of marginalisation as like the state of being outside a circle. The children who fall into one of the above groups, then, find themselves outside. With the focus on educational contexts, it can be argued that the big circle was the school, with smaller circles within being the classrooms. As my research has suggested, the social boundaries of the circles are determined by notions of 'normality', created by members of the society community, and members of the society are socially situated within or outside these boundaries. These notions of 'normality' are socially constructed and hence are likely to change from one setting to another. In other words, what is perceived as 'normal' in one setting might differ in another setting.

Returning to the ideas of Becker (1973), I argue that those who do not fall within the boundaries of 'normality', as created within a particular setting, come to be perceived as 'outsiders' by others and most of the time will experience marginalisation. These boundaries seem fixed, but they are also flexible, depending either on individuals' ability to cross them or on circumstances created within a particular context at a certain time. In other words, though some children were identified as possibly experiencing marginalisation, and therefore lying outside these boundaries, there were still occasions when the same children were found crossing them. The notion of marginalisation here, then, seems not to be a static state.

Becker also argues that deviance varies over time and, in my view, the same could be suggested for marginalisation. However, I am not arguing that marginalisation is simply a 'label' attached to the child. As, I have explained, in the second way of conceptualising marginalisation – when the child is feeling marginalised but most others do not recognise this – it was suggested that marginalisation could indeed be experienced by some of the children even though it was not named as such by others. It was experienced by the children themselves, whether it was considered to exist by others or not. Therefore, rather than thinking about marginalisation in fixed terms it is safer to view it as a loose dynamic concept that varies between contexts and times. Bearing all of this in mind, in what follows I explore how an engagement with the views of students can provide a powerful way of exploring practices and experiences in schools and, therefore, understanding and addressing marginalisation.

Engaging with students' voices

The UN Convention on the Rights of the Child (United Nations, 1989) defines a 'child' as a person below the age of eighteen, unless the relevant laws recognise an earlier age of majority. For the purposes of this book, the term 'children and young people' is used, instead of 'children', since this is perceived as most appropriate, especially when talking about those around the age of fifteen and above. Often in the past children's voices were neglected on the basis that they were not in a position to give accurate information or make judgements (Qvortrup, 1994). However, this is a view that has gradually changed over time and the issue of listening to children is supported by certain official documents. In total, 191 countries were State Parties to the Convention, as of October 1999, and it is the most widely and rapidly ratified human rights treaty in history.

The Convention provides a new vision of children, as being neither the property of their parents, nor helpless objects of charity, but human beings and the subject of their own rights (United Nations, 1989). Within its various Articles, children's rights are discussed in relation to four categories – survival, protection, development and participation – each of which are interrelated (Flekkoy and Kaufman, 1997). In particular, the issue of listening to children is emphasised in Article 12, which reads:

1. States Parties shall assure to the child who is capable of forming his or her own views the right to express those views freely in all matters affecting the child, the view of the child being given due weight in accordance with age and maturity of the child.
2. For this purpose, the child shall in particular be provided with the opportunity to be heard in any judicial and administrative proceedings affecting the child, either directly or through a representative or an appropriate body, in a manner consistent with the procedural rules of natural law.

However, even though Article 12 supports children's right to be heard, the fact that age and maturity of the child are also mentioned leaves a door open for those who had previously rejected this idea precisely for this reason. This is not to deny the role age and maturity play in expressing views, but to emphasise the fact that, regardless of age and maturity, every person's view is equally important.

The government of each country which has ratified the Convention has to submit regular reports on the status of children's rights in its country. However, as Wyse (2001) notes, 'few national institutions or services have adopted a comprehensive approach to children's participation which impacts on children's lives "in all matters affecting the child" (CRC, Article 12)' (p. 209). It seems therefore, that there is a contradiction between practice and what is expressed in the Convention. What should be of more importance is to actually implement what is suggested by the Convention and provide evidence for this implementation. What I am arguing in this book is that the use of the suggested framework can provide evidence of engaging with student's voices and, most importantly, leads to actions and, therefore, an impact on matters that affect them.

Before moving on, however, it is necessary to define what we mean by 'voice'. Alexander (2010) suggests that 'The notion of "voice" is complex and can be used in various ways, reflecting different contexts, aims and beliefs' (p. 144). It could be argued that most people relate voice to what is being expressed through verbal communication. However, in this book, the term involves a broader view, going beyond the notion of what is being said. As Thomson (2008a) argues, voice means 'Having a say, as well as referring to language, emotional compo-nents as well as non-verbal means that are used to express opinions' (p. 4). By adopting this formulation we go beyond the concept of language and refer to other ways of expressing opinions. These include what is *not* been said: that is, silences and what these might mean. As Lewis (2010) argues, 'Listening better includes hearing silence and that silence is not neutral or empty' (p. 20). The framework, through the varying methods and techniques that it employs, aims to bring to the surface all 'voices', starting from the proposition that being heard is one of students' rights.

Apart from the issue of children's right to be heard, what is the value of lis-tening to children in education? Listening to children's voices has been viewed both as an ethical imperative and as a matter of practical utility and efficacy (Davie and Galloway, 1996). Charlton (1996) provides a helpful set of reasons why we should listen to children in schools. He argues that we need to listen to children in our effort to know more about them in order to understand and help them, or because they need to talk about a concern or fear. He proceeds by saying that we also must listen in order to diagnose problems and therefore help children. Last, he points out that we should listen to children because we value their involvement in school affairs and that listening to their views is a way to extend our knowledge of their perceptions of those experiences. In doing so, he argues, we might learn more about our successes and failures, and consider possible changes.

Of all the reasons Charlton suggests, I will focus on his last point about valu-ing students' perspectives as a way to learn more about our own practices and think about possible changes, since I consider this the most important. Indeed, the whole rationale on which the framework is based stems from this belief. In particular, it is based on the assumption that by engaging with students' voices we can reflect on what we offer to them and what they experience, and more importantly think of ways to make changes to improve these experiences. I will also argue that using the framework enables students to go through similar pro-cesses in ways that enable to think about their own behaviour and, in so doing, have an active role in confronting marginalisation.

Going back to Charlton's point about how, through listening to children, we might learn more about our practice, we should note that students may be expected to have different perspectives about issues that are considered. Therefore, they may throw new light on areas under investigation. Daniels and Perry (2003) also mention that, in terms of research, it is possible that children will notice aspects of classroom life that might not be noticed either by teachers or by other adult observers. This position is also shared by Raymond (2001), when she refers to the example of a teacher who has been in a school for twenty-five years. She argues that this teacher felt that the most profound piece of professional developments he had ever been involved in was when he had students in his classroom for observations who reported back to him about what they noticed. In particular, he said that students picked up issues that teachers never observed, such as the fact that he always asked questions to the right side of the class, and that students were intimidated by the fact that he walked up and down the rows during the lessons. Through such examples, it is evident that pupils can identify factors that adults might well overlook. As Prout (2002) points out, including children in research – both as research subjects and as participants – has been shown to reveal many novel aspects of the situations, settings and issues that children were asked about.

However, an opposing view is expressed by Quicke (2003) concerning children's views on learning. He argues that pupils' views are more likely to reflect the dominant view of learning in the school context, and, therefore, researchers should not be surprised if young people's views of learning are conservative. Though Quicke's view may be true in some cases, especially if we accept the fact that children's views are socially constructed, this should not, in my view, be used as an excuse for not using pupils' voices in research or in schools. On the contrary, I would also view this as a challenge to explore whether children's views differ from those of others within the school context. In addition to this, my own experience in schools – both as a researcher and as a practitioner – suggests that where students are given the opportunities to express their views, and feel that these views are valued and respected, it is likely they will 'dare' to express views that might contradict the dominant views of learning in the school. In other words, if the school has managed to create an ethos of trust, students will probably express their honest views. Furthermore, what is important is to look at the details of what the students are expressing, rather than a generic agreement or disagreement with the view of learning in the school.

Accepting children's right to be heard, and the fact that by listening to their voices we have much to learn, is closely related to the way childhood in general is viewed. It is agreed by many authors (e.g. James *et al.*, 1998; Mills and Mills, 2000; Pilcher and Wagg, 1996; Prout and James, 1990) that childhood is socially constructed, and can vary between times and contexts. It is, therefore, best to say that we are talking about childhoods, and not just a single childhood. These childhoods are 'social constructions, cultural components inextricably linked to variables of race, class, culture, gender and time' (Mills, 2000, p. 9). Similarly, I use the term 'students' voices', instead of 'student voice', acknowledging the fact that there is a plurality of voices out there that we need to be engaging with, rather than viewing students' views as being homogenous.

Another important dimension that argues for the necessity to engage with students' voices is expressed by Mitra (2004). Through her research she argues that student voice activities (the term that the author uses) can create meaningful experiences for students, which help to meet fundamental developmental needs. In particular, her research suggests that, by engaging with students' voices growth of agency, belonging and competence was achieved. She argues that this is especially the case for students who otherwise do not find meaning in their school experiences. This particular study is significant in terms of the fact that there is limited research available about the effects of student voice activities on individuals in schools, a theme to which I will return in later chapters.

Although the views of children were often neglected in the past, as I have noted, there are some exceptions to consider. In particular, a number of researchers concerned with pedagogy and general education matters have valued children's ideas and their way of understanding aspects related to education. For instance, Holt (1964), Rowland (1984) and Pollard (1985, 1996) are amongst those who acknowledged the value of engaging with the views of students and incorporated those views in their work. So, as can be seen, the emphasis on students' voices is not a new approach, at least not for researchers. However, certainly, the emphasis and the actual engagement with students' voices in schools is a much more recent phenomenon.

In the English context, it could be argued that the concept of students' voices in schools is relatively well established. This is because it is an area that schools are assessed on through the Office for Standards in Education (OFSTED), which carries out inspections in schools. Until recently, schools have been required to fill in Self-Evaluation Forms (SEF) as part of this inspection and the views of students is an area that they need to demonstrate that they have engaged with. However, in other countries, where no similar procedures exist, the idea of engaging with students' voices may not exist at all. It has to be noted that even in the English context, where schools have to demonstrate how they took into account the views of students, this can sometimes involve a rather tokenistic and superficial approach, rather than being undertaken in a meaningful way. In other words, it is seen more as a 'box-ticking' exercise as part of what schools are expected to do. Therefore, there is space for further developments towards real engagement with the views of children and young people in any context. The framework suggested in this book aims to help towards that direction in schools.

Therefore, even though the idea of listening to children's views has gained ground in recent years internationally, there is still a danger that the approach is used in a rather superficial way, both in schools as well as in research. Fielding (2001) offers a helpful formulation in this respect when he suggests 'a four-fold model which distinguishes between students as sources of data, students as active respondents, students as co-researchers, and students as researchers' (p. 135). These are different levels of student involvement that can be used for school improvement or school self-review, or purely for research purposes. Similar to Fielding's model is Hart's (1992) 'ladder of participation', which is designed to serve as a beginning typology for thinking about the participation of children and young people in projects (see Figure 1.1).

Hart identifies eight levels of young people's participation in projects:

- *Manipulation* is when the adults feel that the end justifies the means. Hart gives an example of preschool children carrying political placards concerning the impact of social policies on children. In this case, children have no understanding of the issues or their actions and therefore this could be described as a way of manipulation.

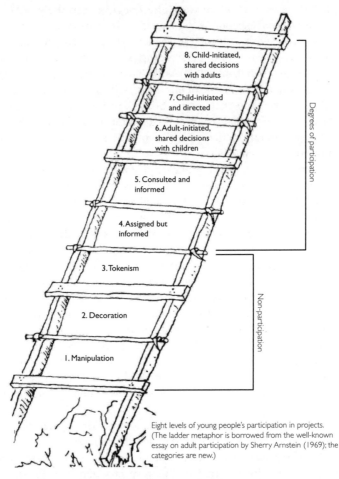

8. Child-initiated, shared decisions with adults

7. Child-initiated and directed

6. Adult-initiated, shared decisions with children

5. Consulted and informed

4. Assigned but informed

3. Tokenism

2. Decoration

1. Manipulation

Degrees of participation

Non-participation

Eight levels of young people's participation in projects. (The ladder metaphor is borrowed from the well-known essay on adult participation by Sherry Arnstein (1969); the categories are new.)

Figure 1.1 The ladder of participation. Source: Hart (1992) Children's participation: From tokenism to citizenship. Innocenti Essays, no. 4. UNICEF International Child Development Centre, Florence (kindly note that the centre is formally known as the International Child Development Centre and the book was published under that imprint).

- *Decoration* is again when children take part in events organised by adults, and have little understanding about the event or no say in its organisation.
- *Tokenism* is when children are given a voice but have little or no choice about the subject or the style of communicating it. One example is when children are used in conference panels but in a rather superficial way.
- *Assigned but informed* is when children are informed about a situation and then asked to participate in the event.
- *Consulted and informed* is when children's views are taken into account in the organising of an event and also informed about the decisions being made.
- *Adult-initiated shared decisions with children* are when a project is started by adults but decisions are made in collaboration with children.
- *Child-initiated and directed* is when children are the ones to start and direct a project and come up with decisions without involving adults in that process.
- *Child-initiated shared decisions with adults* are when the ideas for a project come from children but they share their decisions with adults in order to organise an event or project.

Hart (1992) argues that the main differences between the three lower levels on the ladder, which he calls non-participatory, and the upper five steps, which he calls participatory, is that in all of the upper stages:

- children understand the intentions of the projects
- they know who made decisions about this involvement and why and
- they volunteer for the project after it was made clear to them what the project is about.

Even though Hart's ladder mainly refers to children's and young people's participation in projects, it can be used as a tool for thinking about the way we engage with their voices in any context – either in research projects or for school development. I often use the ladder with practitioners that I work with, and invite them to think about the various activities they use in schools and assign each activity in one of the steps. Both practitioners and I have found it to be a very useful tool in terms of encouraging thinking about how we can make what we offer in schools more participatory. The central idea is to offer students activities that truly promote their active involvement. The higher levels of the ladder can be a useful guide in order to achieve this. In this way, a true engagement with students' voices can be achieved, moving away from superficial or tokenistic approaches. This becomes a crucial issue as we move on to look more specifically at the way students themselves can contribute to inclusive development.

Becoming inclusive

Roaf (2002) argues that researching students' views in relation to inclusive education is a relatively new field, but with great potential in terms of improving children's experience of education on the one hand and teachers' understanding of their pupils on the other hand. This book goes further by arguing that an engagement with students' voices is a way of understanding the notion of inclusion itself. As Ainscow and colleagues (1999) rightly argue, students can be seen as 'hidden voices' that, if listened to, may assist in the development of more inclusive classrooms and schools. The development of the framework is based on this belief and therefore aims to bring those 'hidden voices' to the surface.

Going back to my earlier argument regarding the dangers of thinking about discrete groups in relation to marginalisation, I suggest that a much more useful approach is that of thinking about the notion of diversity. Miles and Ainscow (2011) argue that, even though diversity in education refers to self-evident differences between children and young people, understanding it is far from straightforward. As they suggest, diversity is socially constructed. These views relate to my own argument about marginalisation, that, even though it may sometimes be related to particular groups of learners, it is also a social construction that differs in each unique context and within the interactions between its members.

Diversity is a concept that has been closely linked to the meaning of inclusive education. This idea has been given lots of varying – and some times contrasting – definitions. Florian (1998) has argued that definitions of inclusion tend to focus on different aspects. Some of the definitions, she argues, focus on human interaction, others on valuing diversity, and others on organisational arrangements. Furthermore, Ainscow and colleagues (2006) make a distinction between 'narrow' and 'broad' definitions of inclusion, whereby narrow definitions of inclusion refer to particular groups of students, whereas broader definitions refer to all students and how schools respond to this diversity of learners.

The definitions that I favour are broad. For example, Sebba and Ainscow (1996) define inclusion as

> the process by which a school attempts to respond to all pupils as individuals by reconsidering its curricular organisation and provision. Through this process, the school builds its capacity to accept all pupils from the local community who wish to attend and, in so doing, reduces the need to exclude pupils.
>
> (p. 8)

Here, three key issues emerge: first, the belief that inclusion is not a state but a process concerning all children; second, emphasis on the restructuring of curricular organisation and provision; and last, through this definition, the perception of processes of exclusion as informative to the movement of inclusion. These key issues relate to my ideas about marginalisation and, consequently, to the development of the framework. In other words, the framework can be seen as a way of directing us towards various ways of reconstructing what is on offer in schools, in such a way so to avoid marginalising anyone and, therefore, to include *all*.

Even though the position I adopt relate to such broad definitions, it is necessary to examine how inclusion is understood generally, not least because it is mentioned as part of the subtitle of this book. Furthermore, since the book is intended to be used by practitioners as well as by academics, it is essential to understand how inclusion is perceived by both groups. Ainscow and colleagues (2006) refer to a typology of six ways of thinking about inclusion: these refer to inclusion as a concern with disabled students and others categorised as 'having special educational needs'; a response to disciplinary exclusion; about all groups vulnerable to exclusion; the promotion of the school for all; 'education for all'; and a principled approach to education (p. 15). This formulation emerged from a collaborative action research project carried out with practitioners in schools in England, and therefore some of the above formulations may not apply internationally. For example, inclusion as being a response to disciplinary exclusion might not have any meaning in some contexts, since this might be a practice that does not exist in a given country. Nevertheless, the typology is very helpful in terms of thinking about how inclusion can be viewed.

The 'principled approach to education' suggested by Ainscow and his colleagues emphasises the fact that inclusion is a never-ending process concerned with all children and young people, focusing on their presence, participation and achievement in schools. This approach is also consistent with the broader view of inclusion that has been adopted by many other key writers in the field (e.g. Ainscow, 1999; Armstrong *et al*., 2000; Ballard, 1997; Booth and Ainscow, 1998; Mittler, 2000), who explicitly point out that inclusion is concerned with any kind of marginalisation that might be experienced by any child, regardless of whether this is perceived as being about notions of special needs or not. Such broad definitions, with their emphasis on restructuring schools in order to accept all children, relate directly to my own work and the proposed framework in this book. Therefore, viewing inclusion as the process by which a school attempts to embrace the diversity among learners, the suggested framework can be viewed as one of the ways that can facilitate this process by making sure that issues that relate to marginalisation are identified and addressed.

Though definitions are important in enabling us to develop clarity around issues under discussion, Mordal and Stromstad (1998) raise another important concern, with a focus on special educational needs:

> Whether we use the terms 'integration', 'inclusion', 'adapted education' or 'one school for all', for any particular child, we still have to ask: is this child really included as a full-member of the school community, or have we only made superficial adaptations which leave the child just as isolated as in a special class or special school?

(p. 106)

Similarly, I extend these questions in relation to any student that might feel marginalised in a given context. Addressing such questions, other issues emerge; for example: Who is in a position to provide these answers? Whose voice should be heard to explore the above issues?

Corbett and Slee (2000) argue that 'Within an inclusive education there is a plurality of voices devoid of existing hierarchies of status and privilege' (p. 135). They go on to suggest that directly listening to marginalised and excluded people themselves might give great insight. In this sense, marginalised people's voices should have a central role in the process of inclusion. Importantly, however, the use of the framework goes a step further and engages with *all* students' voices, given the fact that who is marginalised is not straightforward, as indicated by the four ways of conceptualising marginalisation. By focusing on *all* students' voices through the framework process, the aim is to identify whether what is happening in schools is truly enabling *all* learners to be included, and if not, define ways in which this can happen.

The rationale behind the framework also relates to what Clark and colleagues (1995) refer to as the 'organisational paradigm' of inquiry in relation to special education. Difficulties in education have been explained in terms of two competing perspectives (Skrtic, 1986). The first of these – sometimes referred to as an 'individual pupil view' – is where difficulties experienced with learning are interpreted in terms of individual characteristics. This relates to what has also been called the medical model of disability, which sees the problem in the person and their impairment, rather than on the system and its need for restructuring (Rieser, 2011). On the other hand, the 'organisational paradigm', as Clark and colleagues (1995) argue, is founded on two assumptions: first, that special education is the consequence of inadequacies in the current state of development of mainstream schools; and, second, that there are ways which should be found to make schools more capable of responding to the diversity of students. Clark and her colleagues go on argue that research which follows this paradigm 'is directed at identifying what features within schools facilitate such responses and what processes can be initiated which would bring those features about' (p. 79). This different way of thinking leads directly to the idea of inclusive education, with its emphasis on restructuring schools in response to students' diversity. Therefore, the rationale on which the framework has been developed follows this 'organisational paradigm' and, in particular, views the issue of listening to children as one of the processes which could bring to the surface features that are important for the successful development of more inclusive forms of education. I should add here that the development of the framework relates to the ideas presented in the Index for Inclusion (Booth and Ainscow, 2002), a school review instrument that places particular emphasis on the importance of analysing contextual factors in schools in order to address barriers to learning and participation of students.

Many of the ideas in this book were influenced by those writers who refer specifically to the idea of listening to students in relation to inclusion. For example,

Mittler (2000) defines inclusion as being 'about everyone having opportunities for choice and self-determination. In education, it means listening to and valuing what children have to say, regardless of age or labels' (p. viii). Therefore, it is about not just listening to children's and young people's voices, but going a step further and truly valuing what they have to say. Barton (1997) goes further, defining inclusion as being 'about listening to unfamiliar voices, being open, empowering all members and about celebrating "difference" in dignified ways . . . Inclusive experience is about learning to live with one another' (p. 233). Therefore, it can be argued that, through this process of listening to children's and young people's voices, we are empowering them, as well as recognising that they are valued members of a community. Most importantly, through this process we are learning to live with one another, which is central to a commitment to inclusion.

Therefore, taking this broader view of inclusion as being concerned with any learner that might experience marginalisation, I am arguing that in order to truly be inclusive we should take notice of *all* learners' voices. Alternatively, as I have argued elsewhere, listening to children's and young people's voices is in itself a manifestation of being inclusive (Messiou, 2006b). This is particularly important, especially for researchers. If we are only focusing on those learners perceived as having special educational needs, or others who have been given some sort of label, through our own actions as researchers we may be reinforcing certain stereotypes associated with those categories of groups of learners (Messiou, 2002). For example, researchers who, in choosing interview participants, single out individual students who have been defined as having special educational needs may lead to further reinforcement of students' perceptions of difference. Similarly, practitioners may act in such ways too with the above consequences.

The framework

On the basis of the arguments I have presented so far, and drawing on evidence from my research engagement in schools, the framework for addressing marginalisation and promoting inclusion was developed. It is intended to be used by researchers who are working in collaboration with teachers and students in schools. It can also be used by teachers themselves in schools, or, indeed, by students who take on the roles of researchers or co-researchers. The examples provided in the following chapters demonstrate how it has been used by members of staff and students in schools, as well as by me as a researcher, in various school contexts, both primary and secondary.

The approach that I am suggesting through the use of this framework moves away from easy to follow recipes. Though it does suggest a step-by-step process, in all steps the necessity to stop and think, and further reflect on existing practices, is highlighted. This is not to say that it is a difficult approach to use, but rather to illustrate that it is not a straightforward process. It is also important to recognise that there is a degree of unpredictability involved, since what each step reveals is based on what the students bring to the surface, which is likely to be different between school contexts as well as within different classrooms in the same school.

The framework predominantly focuses on students' roles, as well as teachers' role, and most importantly the collaboration between them, in addressing marginalisation. This is not to ignore the importance that other factors within a given context may have on creating and addressing marginalisation, such as the structures within the society, the curriculum or the impact of policies on the everyday lives of teachers and children and young people in schools. However, the point that I am making is that by engaging with students' voices, in collaboration with teachers, there is potential for change, especially in regards to marginalisation at the school level.

The framework is intended to be used flexibly, rather than followed rigidly. It consists of four steps and involves a cyclical process, as illustrated in Figure 1.2.

In what follows, each of the steps is introduced briefly, since the following chapters deal with each step in greater detail.

Step 1: Opening doors: enabling voices to emerge

In this first step, groups of members of staff – in some cases with the support of external researchers – work collaboratively with children and young people in order to engage with their views in an authentic way. The idea here is that various methods are used to allow voices, and issues that might lead to marginalisation of students in the schools, to emerge. Methods to be used can include

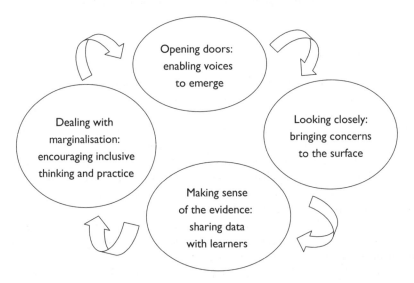

Figure 1.2 A framework for promoting inclusion.

observations, interviews, visual images, drawing, role-play and sociometric measures. All these methods place students at the centre of the process, viewing them as active participants rather than as subjects that will give us information. In some contexts, the adults involved in this first step are the classroom teachers; elsewhere it may be others working in schools, as for example, teaching assistants or specialist support staff. Through this step, as its title suggests, the aim is to use such approaches that will allow students to express their true views and concerns about their experiences in schools.

Step 2: Looking closely: bringing concerns to the surface

This step involves the close examination of the information gained during the previous step in order to identify those individuals who may be experiencing some form of marginalisation in the school, as well as issues that may be leading to their marginalisation. Practitioners, researchers or students who act as co-researchers, having helped to collect information in the first step, have to look closely at this information. Through this process their assumptions may be challenged, especially if their colleagues are used to bring a critical perspective to the process. At this step, groups of students are not usually taking part; it is just the practitioners looking at the information gained, unless students acted as co-researchers. Again, the way that this is done may vary from one context to another, especially given the time limits that exist. However, ideally, members of staff should get together at some stage and share this information and the initial information that is emerging about particular students and about specific issues as well. Part of this step is to single out data and information that will be used to inform the following step of the framework. Decisions on what kind of data and information to single out entail ethical dimensions that need to be taken into account.

Step 3: Making sense of the evidence: sharing data with learners

This focuses attention directly on issues of marginalisation that have emerged through the previous step. It involves dialogue between adults and students, who all become learners as part of this process. At this stage, it will be crucial to ensure the anonymity of individual pupils. In other words, it should be ensured that when sharing data with students no one is in a position to understand who has brought up the issue, and this should be made clear to everyone from the beginning. Therefore, names of individuals who we might think might experience marginalisation, based on the information we got from the activities, should not be mentioned, since this would be unethical. Rather, we should focus on issues related to marginalisation and use those as a way to make students reflect about their own experiences, as well as about their classmates' feelings and experiences.

Step 4: Dealing with marginalisation: encouraging inclusive thinking and practice

This last step can be seen as overlapping with the previous one. In sharing data, and issues that have emerged through the data collection, students are most likely to start making suggestions about how to address some of these issues. However, of course, the most important aspect is acting on these issues, and, consequently, truly confronting marginalisation. In the light of the evidence that has been analysed, actions have to be determined in order to address issues of marginalisation. Again, this will involve collaboration between students and teachers.

As I have explained, the framework involves a cyclical process and it is likely that at the end of the final step other issues will emerge that need to be further explored. It must also be remembered that marginalisation is a complex multi-faceted notion, and therefore it should not be assumed that following the four-step process will lead to the elimination of all forms of marginalisation within a particular context. However, my experience has been that, once such an approach is embedded in a school's work, teachers are likely to be more sensitive towards listening to what children and young people say and sharing concerns with them in order to find solutions. In addition to this, both practitioners and students can change their attitudes, which in effect can act as a way of preventing marginalisation of individuals in the future. Therefore, this framework should be viewed in relation to inclusion as being a never-ending process and can therefore be used as a way of promoting inclusion.

In the following chapter an example of how the framework was used in one school is presented in order to bring to light the process that can be followed. As will be seen through the example, the four steps overlap to some extent. Even though the steps are presented diagrammatically as being separate, it is important to keep this in mind, so as to avoid seeing the whole process as a mechanical activity. The overlapping nature of the steps will be further discussed in the final chapter, where the framework is refined.

Summary and conclusion

In this chapter I have explained that marginalisation is complex and can appear in many subtle forms within schools. Therefore, a move away from views that relate marginalisation to particular groups of learners is needed. In doing so, an engagement with students' voices seems to be essential for understanding and addressing marginalisation in school contexts. In this way, more inclusive contexts can be developed.

A framework for promoting inclusion by engaging with students' voices has been outlined. This involves a four-step approach that is intended to be used flexibly. Each of the steps are explored in subsequent chapters.

Chapter 2

Using the framework

An example of how the framework was used in one particular school is discussed in this chapter, in order for the reader to get a holistic view of the processes involved. As I have explained, the framework can be used by researchers, by practitioners or by students who take the role of co-researchers.

The example used here is from a school where teachers collaborated with me as a researcher. It should be noted, however, that my involvement was kept to the minimum, since the aim was to explore how teachers in a school context can use the framework to engage with students' voices.

Whereas this chapter focuses on the overall process of using the framework, more detailed guidance for each of the steps is provided in the chapters that follow. There examples from different school contexts are provided in order to demonstrate how each step can be approached in different ways and reinforce the idea that the framework should be used flexibly to suit particular circumstances.

Background

The project took place in a primary school with 210 students and fourteen members of teaching staff. I was invited to give a presentation at the school that related to issues of inclusion and exclusion, linked to themes of the European Year for Combating Poverty and Social Exclusion. I was asked to focus particularly on school issues, which led me to connect my presentation to the argument of Pierson (2001), who argues that:

> Social exclusion focuses on social relations and the extent to which people are able to participate in social affairs and attain sufficient power to influence decisions that affect them.
>
> (p. 2)

Based on this argument, I suggested to the teachers that by engaging with students' voices we are empowering and preparing them to be actively engaged in decisions that affect their future lives. At the same time I took the opportunity to offer the framework process as one way of engaging with students' views.

During the presentation I also explained the rationale for the framework and gave examples of methods for data collection and data analysis, albeit in very general terms.

Following my presentation the teachers had the opportunity to clarify any issues related to the framework. This allowed me to make it very clear to them that they had the flexibility to use it in such a way so as to fit their schedules and the realities of their school context. As a result, the headteacher and some of her staff became interested in the process and decided to use it as a whole school approach in order to identify and address issues of marginalisation.

One of the reasons I chose the particular example to illustrate the process is because the whole school used it and, ideally, this should be happening whenever possible. In addition to this, the practitioners used the framework in this particular school with minimum input from me as a researcher. Through this example, I wanted to show the potential of the framework as a strategy for whole school development.

The use of the framework

One of the first issues that the practitioners in the particular school had to address was how to present the approach to their students. As it was a primary school, and given the fact that the framework would be incorporated into the daily plans of the school, the teachers quite rightly agreed that there was no need to refer to the actual framework, or to the issue of marginalisation. In fact, though this was their main area of concern, at the same time they were interested in finding out about various other issues in the school. The headteacher explained that each of the teachers introduced the use of the activities of the first step to their class, using a version of the following statement:

> All the teachers in the school would like to know how you feel about your experiences here in the school. Therefore, we discussed and agreed that for this week we will be doing some activities that will enable you to tell us what you feel about your school and the things that we do here. So, we want to learn from you and see how we can make changes to improve your experience.

A statement like this was certainly true and I agreed with the teachers that using the word 'marginalisation' would not add anything in their case. This reinforces the point that, even though the framework is particularly concerned with marginalisation, it can be used as a way of evaluating students' experiences in the school in a broader sense. This was what the particular school decided to do.

The actual processes used in the school involved the four steps, as follows:

Step 1: Opening doors: enabling voices to emerge

The school decided to dedicate a one-week period when all teachers would be engaged with data collection through the use of specific methods. In particular, they chose to use a series of techniques that I had developed in my earlier work. These included message in a bottle, the communication box, sociograms, visual images and observations. Detailed explanations of each of these methods and guidance on the practicalities that need to be taken into account in using them are provided in the following chapter. Here a brief description of what happened in the school is offered in order to bring to life the process of using the framework.

Each teacher used some of the data collection methods at a time within the week that he/she felt it was most appropriate. In this way, they were able to incorporate the activities into their daily plans. All of them chose to use the 'message in a bottle' technique. This is an idea that I had adapted from Davies's (2000) work, where she had used it to explore democratic processes within schools. In my earlier work, I had decided to use the technique to bring to the surface voices of concern. It involves asking students to write down a message saying what they would like to change at school, if they could change one thing. The teachers used the technique with their whole classes, where the students were given pieces of paper with prompts to write their messages (Figure 2.1). They were given the option to write these messages either anonymously or not.

As a follow-up activity, the teachers also used the communication box activity. This involved a box that was placed in a central point of the school where students could post their letters/messages, if they wanted to express a view in that way. Again, the school gave the students the choice of posting these messages anonymously or not. It was explained to the students that they could post their messages as and when they felt like doing this. Though there was

Message in a bottle

If I could change something in my school (something I do not like), what would it be?

I would like to ....

....

....

Name: .... Class: ....

Figure 2.1 Message in a bottle materials.

one-week limit to post these messages – since the practitioners wanted to gather all the information and analyse it – in fact, the box remained in the school until the end of the school year.

The other activity that was used involved the use of sociometric measures. This is a well-established research technique which explores relationships among members of a group (Moreno, 1934; Wasserman and Faust, 1994). Students were told at the beginning of this activity that teachers wanted to find out what children's preferences were, in order to use them for future seating plans and organisation of groups for activities in the school. So the students were asked to write down on a piece of paper the names of three children they would like to work with in the class, and three they would like to play with. It was made clear to the students that they would not have to share their nominations with anyone else.

Some of the teachers also used visual images approaches, more specifically the idea of photo voice, which involves students in taking photographs and explaining their significance (Wang et al., 1998). In particular, the teachers wanted to explore learning aspects within the school. With this in mind, they asked students to take pictures within their classrooms that showed what helps them with their learning and what makes it difficult for them. Students were put into groups of four and were given a camera for a whole day. So, for example, one group of students took the picture in Figure 2.2 to show that what helps them is the use of real objects for solving maths problems.

Figure 2.2 A picture taken by students showing that the use of real objects helps them with their learning.

Then each group had to prepare posters with these pictures and write captions demonstrating what they felt about what was happening in the class.

Step 2: Looking closely: bringing concerns to the surface

Once the data were collected each teacher examined them, on their own in the first place. So, for example, for the sociometric measures, each practitioner transferred students' preferences onto a table and highlighted those students who were not chosen by anyone (Figure 2.3).

The practitioners explained that filling in these tables with students' nominations brought some surprises for them. As they explained, on some occasions they were finding out that students whom they perceived as very popular did not get many nominations, whereas others who they thought would not get nominations did get some in the end. Most importantly, they were surprised in two respects: first, that on some occasions there were many students who received no nominations at all; and, second, who those students were.

The messages in a bottle, as well as the messages posted in the communication box, were all gathered together and typed up by the headteacher. The reason for typing up the comments was to ensure complete anonymity of the students when their comments were shared with the staff during the next step. Since teachers become so familiar with students' handwriting they would possibly be in a position to recognise whose message they were reading. In addition, though some students were identifying themselves by providing their full names, and others were only identifying the class they belonged to, the headteacher decided not to use this information at all. The reason for doing this, she explained, was

Names	David	Andy	John	Peter	Luke	Philip	George	Nick	Andrew	Brian	Mark	Joseph	Mohammed	Lewis	Janine	Mary	Liz	Ann	Janet	Sophie	Fiona	Nancy
David			✱						✱	✱												
Andy	✱								✱	✱												
John				✱		✱						✱										
Peter			✱	✱								✱										
Luke			✱					✱				✱										
Philip		✱	✱									✱										
George	✱	✱	✱																			
Nick			✱							✱											✱	
Andrew	✱	✱	✱																			
Brian							✱											✱	✱			
Mark		✱	✱									✱										
Joseph		✱	✱	✱																		
Mohammed		✱	✱									✱										
Lewis		✱	✱							✱												
Janine																		✱	✱		✱	
Mary	✱																✱	✱			✱	
Liz																		✱		✱	✱	
Ann												✱							✱			✱
Janet												✱						✱				✱
Sophie																		✱	✱			✱
Fiona						✱												✱	✱		✱	
Nancy																		✱	✱	✱		
	3	0	8	9	3	2	1	2	1	4	1	6	2	0	2	0	1	5	6	3	3	4

Figure 2.3 Table indicating students' nominations.

to avoid having teachers focusing only on what students from their class had said. In other words, she felt that students' comments should be shared with everyone in order to make them think about what was happening in the school in general. The headteacher then examined all the messages and picked out those that she thought to be of particular concern, or interesting for further discussion with the teachers. For example, Figure 2.4 lists some of the messages she identified for further consideration.

The headteacher explained that deciding on which messages to be shared with the rest of the staff, and, indeed, with students at a later stage, was not a straightforward process. For example, there were some messages that were making reference to particular individual students or individual teachers, such as:

- Chris, from Mrs M.'s class, hits all the children.
- Mrs K. does not let us go for a break, or to leave school, when the bell rings because she wants us to finish our work first.

The headteacher told me that they had not asked children to avoid mentioning other students' or teachers' names. (All names used in the book are pseudonyms in order to ensure anonymity.) She added that, on reflection, it would have been more ethically appropriate if they had. Nevertheless, she had found it helpful to read messages that were revealing about some students and teachers (ethics are discussed in more detail later on). For example, concerns about the behaviour of one student were revealed in a number of messages. Up to that point there were no concerns about the behaviour of this particular individual. In the same way, she noticed that many children were expressing a specific view about one particular teacher.

In the end, the headteacher decided to delete all the names from such messages and to use them with all teachers in order to make them think carefully about their own practices. In other words, rather than identifying individuals, she considered it to be a much more useful approach to use those messages as a way of enabling teachers to reflect on their own behaviours and practices, as well as on what was happening in the school more generally. In those cases

---

- We would like to do more work in our groups (rather than working individually).
- Some teachers come late to class and we waste time from our lessons.
- I want, and I want it so much, to be a member of the School Council.
- I want to have friends to play with.
- I want the games rota to change during break time.

Figure 2.4 Students' messages from 'message in a bottle' and 'communication box' activities.

where reference was made to a particular student – as was the case in the above message (*Chris, from Mrs M.'s class, hits all the children*) – she also alerted individual teachers on a one-to-one basis, in order to be more vigilant about these students' behaviour. However, she did not want to mention the names in front of all the teachers, since her instinct was that this might lead to labelling of individual students.

Finally, the students who took photographs were asked to use them to design posters that conveyed their thoughts. One of the teachers put these on display in the classroom for the other students to look at. In addition, she organised another session at which further discussions took place with a particular focus on the issues that were emerging through the photographs.

Once again all the posters – as well as the key points that were identified through these discussions – were gathered together in order that they could be shared with other teachers. This material, the information from the sociometric measures and the selected messages from the communication box and the message in a bottle were eventually discussed at a staff meeting. Later some of this material was also shared with the students as part of the next step.

Step 3: Making sense of the evidence: sharing data with learners

As I explained in the previous chapter, though the framework is presented in the form of separate steps, these are at the same time overlapping. For instance, in the previous step, practitioners could have got together to look at the data, in pairs for example, in order to make sense of it. In the particular school this did not occur, owing to time constraints, but ideally this should have happened. On the other hand, some of the information was shared with other students through the discussion of the visual images, for example. The information that each group of students gathered was shared with all the students in their class and further discussions took place at the time. Similarly, it could be argued that those practitioners who looked at the data on their own started making sense of the data. It can be seen, therefore, that the sharing of the information with others and a deeper level of analysis can start during the previous step, at least to some extent.

Whereas the previous step focuses on identifying areas of concerns, or identifying individuals who might experience marginalisation within a school context, this third step focuses more on looking at the details and understanding the complexities of the data through a more collaborative process. The potential of this step is that it engages with multiple voices and, therefore, allows for and stimulates further reflection on everyone's part.

As I have explained, in the particular school the data and information were shared with members of staff during a staff meeting. Three sources of data were debated: the key points from the posters and the posters themselves; the tables summarising the sociometric data; and selected items from the message in a bottle and the communication box activities. In this way, the teachers were in a position to discuss their initial understandings, as well as to see what their colleagues brought to the table.

During an interview, the headteacher told me that the discussions that evolved during the staff meeting were really interesting. In particular, all the teachers were clearly very interested in looking at what the information meant and, in so doing, discussing possible explanations for the students' views. She explained that the method that created most discussion was the sociometric measures. What was significant in this particular context, being a relatively small school, was that the teachers knew most of the children in the various classes. Therefore, they could all relate to the information about the students' preferences. Consequently, they were in a position, to some extent at least, to discuss individual students and the nominations they received. Specifically, the teachers were surprised at how many students were not chosen by anyone, neither to play with nor to work with.

The validity of this particular method is discussed in Chapter 4, and this issue was also discussed with the teachers during the presentation that I did in the school. In particular, it was emphasised that the results from the sociometric measures should not be taken at face value in the sense that children's views may change rapidly, even within a single day. However, what was very interesting was that the evidence clearly provoked discussion and reflection amongst the staff. In particular, it directed their attention to individual students who possibly had not been of any concern to them before.

The discussions led the teachers to decide that they wanted to find out more about particular students. At the same time, they wanted to explore whether the information gained from the sociograms was a true reflection of what was happening in the school with regard to particular individuals. Initially, they wanted to focus on all those students who got either no nominations or only one nomination. This meant focusing on a relatively large number of students, which would make the collection of more data difficult and time-consuming.

In consultation with me, the staff finally decided to focus only on those students who have not received any nominations – a total of nineteen students – which made it more manageable. As a result of their discussions, they decided to shadow these individuals during break times to find out if they truly had no one to play with. In particular, they developed what they called a single diary of observations for the group of students. This had a page for each student who was identified as having no nominations from his/her classmates. Whichever teacher was on duty outside in the playground focused attention on one or two of these students. If they saw something of interest they would note it down in the notebook.

For some students, it emerged that there were no real issues since they were included in the games that the children were playing, whereas for others it emerged that what the sociograms revealed was confirmed. For example, it was found out that some of the individuals who were not nominated by anyone were seen to be mainly on their own during playtimes. The teachers explained to me that they noticed that, at times, some of these students were actively attempting to be included in games. Sometimes this led the teachers to intervene. For example, one teacher explained:

> I was watching this girl in the playground – who had no nominations from her classmates neither for playing with her or to work with her. She approached one group of girls that were playing a game and she wanted to take part in their game too. She started intervening, and clearly the others did not like it as she was spoiling their game. It seemed to me that she did not know how to approach them and the way she was doing it was inappropriate. I approached and I suggested to her to wait until they finish that round of the game and then ask them to join in. She did that and the others were happy with that.

The teachers remained vigilant, however, knowing the impact that a teacher's presence might have on students' behaviour. This led them to keep checking that the particular girl had friends to play with at playtime.

It has to be noted that I was not present at the staff meeting where the decision was made to adopt the diary of observations. This approach emerged out of the conversations that the teachers had during the meeting, taking into account what they felt to be feasible within the particular school. This reinforces my argument that the framework should not be seen as a recipe to follow. Rather, the specifics of each context, and the creativity of members of staff, should determine how to approach issues that emerge.

Later, information gathered through the message in a bottle, the communication box and the visual images, as well as extracts from some observations, were shared with students within some of the classes. Here the aim was to stimulate wider debate within the school community and, in so doing, gain a better understanding of students' experiences. Of course, the more sensitive information gained through sociometric measures was not to be shared with the students.

One particular teacher did a session with her whole class in which she shared some of the messages that were of concern to her and some of the observation notes of playground interactions. Specifically, she divided the class into groups of four and asked them to look at the messages mentioned in Figure 2.4, as well as the observation notes presented in Figure 2.5. Then students were asked to think about a set of questions (see Figure 2.6) in relation to this incident.

The idea of using this approach came about through a discussion the teacher had with me. I suggested what I had done in another school when I was sharing information with students, as part of an intervention phase (Messiou, 2008a). More examples of this approach are provided in a later chapter. What is important here is that such observation notes stimulated discussions among both students and teachers.

Many students from one class are playing a game. A girl, from the same class, is standing there looking at the other students. She tries to join at some point by asking one of her classmates. The other girl tells her that she cannot join. She approaches another student and the other student tells her the same. In the end, they ask her to be part of the game by being the observer letting them know if anyone breaks the rules. In other words, they invent a role for her but she is not really participating in the game.

Figure 2.5 Observation notes that were used with a whole group of students.

- How do you think this student feels?
- Do you think what has happened is fair?
- Has anyone been in a similar situation at school? Can you give us an example?
- What could be done so that such incidents are avoided?

Figure 2.6 Set of questions that students had to address in their groups.

The teacher went on to explain that, during the class discussion, her students gave other examples in which students were marginalised in the school, both in the playground and in the class. Most importantly, she commented, this had led some of the students to think about their own behaviours and how these might be altered in order to address issues of marginalisation within the school.

In other school contexts, members of staff decided to share the information with students and other practitioners at the same time, as explained in Chapter 5. This reinforces my argument that the framework should be used flexibly in such a way that it fits in with the realities of each context.

Step 4: Dealing with marginalisation: encouraging inclusive thinking and practice

This final step of the framework, as with the previous two steps, should be seen as overlapping and interconnected with what previously occurred. For example, when the teacher shared the information with the children in her class and asked them to find ways so that nobody feels left out, this was definitely planting the seeds of inclusive thinking in their minds. Of course, suggestions may be far from reality and the challenge is to turn intentions into changes in behaviour. The key factor, therefore, is to make sure that suggestions move beyond rhetoric and are turned into action. That is why the close monitoring of what is actually happening in schools, by teachers and in collaboration with students, is so essential.

A number of actions were taken in this particular school as a result of the engagement with the framework. Some of the changes were at a general level, in respect to school policy and practices, whereas some of the changes were at the individual level, in terms of both teachers and students. So, as I have mentioned, a number of students were expressing concerns about the fact that they did not have friends to play with. What the staff decided to do was to work with the school council in order to address this issue. The council members, each being representatives of their classes, came up with the idea that individual students should take on the role of friendship facilitators during playtime. Their task would be to make sure that those children who did not have anyone to play with could find some friends and join in some games. The school council decided that they would ask for volunteers to take on this role and that it would be very important that all the students should be made aware about the role of these individuals. Furthermore, in order that these students would be easily identified by other students in the playground, they came up with the idea that they should wear a colourful band on their arm. As the teachers explained, this system worked well and it was noticeable how children felt more comfortable approaching the student facilitators and asking for their help to find friends, rather than telling the teachers. However, it has to be noted that this does not mean that all problems were addressed through this approach; the teachers continued to observe the individual students that they had targeted through the use of sociometric measures. Some of them, as they found out, managed to create friendships through the facilitators, and, therefore, became more included during playtimes; whereas other attempts were not deemed to be successful. On those occasions, the teachers felt that they had to intervene at a more individual level.

For example, one specific girl was identified as experiencing marginalisation in the school. Though she tried to make friends by approaching the friendship facilitators, this was not successful, or was partially successful only when the facilitators were present – which in effect means that they were not successful. The teachers then felt that they had to intervene at a more personal level. The teacher of this particular class decided to talk to a group of girls that she thought could be understanding about how this girl felt been excluded from all their games. It emerged from the discussion that the reason the girls did not want to play with this particular student was because they had seen lice in her hair and wanted to avoid her. The teacher looked more closely on the girl's hair and indeed there were lice. She spoke to the girl individually and through the discussion it emerged that, although she had given her parents the leaflets that the school distributed in regards to lice, they never seemed to pay any attention. The teacher then asked the mother to come to the school and explained why this was so important, and how it had an effect on her daughter's social participation at school. The mother understood the significance of this and promised to make sure that she would address the problem. Later, the teacher had another conversation with the group of girls and noticed that indeed the girls started playing with the other student.

Another issue that emerged through the use of the framework related to the use of group work, in particular, that students wanted to work more in groups. This was seen by the teachers as a way of addressing marginalisation of some individual students during lessons. However, as the headteacher explained, it emerged through the discussions in the staff meeting that her colleagues had differing views regarding what group work means, and, most importantly, how it can be put into practice in such a way so as to make sure that all children participate effectively. Therefore, the head organised a staff development session about cooperative learning and group work, to make sure that the teachers were clear about how they could put this into practice with a particular focus on making sure that every student was actively participating. For example, it emerged that some teachers thought that group work simply meant having students sitting in groups, just asking them to discuss as a group and agree on a common answer. They were not aware, for example, of the different roles that members of the group can take and the importance of the common task for the group (Baloche, 1998; Cohen *et al.*, 1999; Fuchs *et al.*, 2000; Johnson *et al.*, 1993; Kagan, 1992). By learning about the principles behind cooperative learning, as well as the practical issues associated with using it, the teachers were in a position to allow individual students to participate in the learning process in a way that had not been achieved before.

Reflections on the process

As we saw, some of the changes introduced in this particular context were not very difficult to implement. No doubt many schools are already using such practices and would, therefore, find these quite simplistic and even common sense. So why is there a need to go through this process of collecting and engaging with the views of students? What is the importance of using the framework and what does it add to the usual ways in which schools seek to refine their ways of working?

What I am arguing through this example – as well as through the examples that follow in the next chapters – is that the use of the framework enabled these teachers (and to some extent students) to think more critically in regards to what is happening in their school and what particular individuals are experiencing. By using the framework, teachers and students stopped and reflected on what was emerging from the data. Furthermore, they stopped and thought about *why* some students were expressing specific views and, most importantly, *how* they could address some of the issues that were brought to the surface. In this sense, the process created an 'interruption' of the sort described by Ainscow and colleagues (2006) and, in so doing, threw light on overlooked possibilities for involving students who were previously being marginalised. Collaboration in terms of analysing information was crucial to this process in order that, through the use of the framework, reflective analysis can be achieved. Similar to Hart's (2000) 'Innovative Thinking', my framework aims to assist participants in moving beyond existing perceptions and understandings. As we have seen, at the heart of this process lies careful listening to what the students are saying.

In the particular school, as the headteacher said to me during an interview, the teachers became more alert and sensitive towards students' experiences in the school. She explained:

> The teachers used to be on duty during break time in a rather superficial way. In a way, an adult's presence in the playground is a sort of reassurance for the children. However, many times teachers only pay attention to problems that might arise in the playground, like fighting among students, and try to intervene when necessary.

Through the use of this framework teachers became more attentive towards individual students and, in a way, towards what was happening in the playground in a more general sense. Changes in thinking and attitudes are difficult to measure, however, but changes in behaviours can be observed. As the headteacher explained, she had noted a change in most of the teachers' behaviours, which, she believed, had resulted from their use of the framework and the discussions that it provoked.

As I explained at the beginning of this chapter, my intention was to give the reader one example of how the framework has been used in a particular context. Some of the details of the implementation of the methods of data collection have not been discussed extensively here, since the focus was on giving an overview of the process. More details about each of these techniques presented – and additional ones that can be used in the first step of the framework – are found in the following chapter.

Before moving on, however, it is important to clarify some issues that are of importance before getting started with the framework, namely:

- How should the framework be introduced?
- Who should facilitate the process?
- When should the framework be used and for how long?
- What are the ethical considerations that need to be kept in mind?

These issues will help with getting organised before using the framework in a school context. They mainly apply when practitioners or students as co-researchers use the framework with minimum input from researchers. At the same time, these are issues that will also be relevant to researchers who adopt the framework.

How should the framework be introduced?

My experience suggests that it is preferable that the framework be used as part of a whole school approach, as was the case in my example. However, I have also witnessed examples of individual teachers who have used the framework effectively on their own as a way of understanding what is happening in their classes. In addition, as I will show in later chapters, students themselves can take on the role of co-researchers, using the framework to tackle issues across a whole school, or within specific classes or year groups.

Right from the decision to introduce the framework into a school there are major ethical issues to address. For example, is it necessary to tell those involved, including students, that the focus will be on marginalisation and, by implication, on certain individuals assumed to be vulnerable? If we do not give enough information to the students about the purpose of the framework, how ethical is the approach?

My position on these challenging issues is based on my experiences of using the framework in a range of schools. This leads me to conclude that there is not a simple answer. How much information is given to the students depends on their age, the purposes of using the approach and who is leading the process. Generally speaking my experience is that, when using the framework, primary school teachers do not give a great deal of information to the children and would certainly not use the word 'marginalisation', precisely for ethical reasons, as well as because of the complex nature of the term. Indeed, I feel that using the term could do more harm than good (Messiou, 2003). Certainly, the school in the above example did not use the word 'marginalisation' at any time. As I mentioned earlier, teachers emphasised the fact that they were interested in finding out how students feel about their experiences in the school. On the other hand, in some secondary schools the term 'marginalisation' was used and the diagram of the framework itself was shown to students to make the process more explicit. In one school in particular, where a group of students took on the role of co-researchers, they were very honest in terms of what the project was about (marginalisation) and what they were trying to achieve. This is ideal in terms of ethical issues; however, it might not be appropriate with younger children for the reasons mentioned above.

My advice, therefore, is that, even if practitioners do not share the rationale and whole process of the framework in advance with students, they definitely have to be very clear from the beginning why they are asking students to do particular activities; for example, by acting in similar ways to the teachers in the school in this chapter, who explained to the students that they wanted to find out their views about the school in order to improve their experiences.

Even though written consent might not be necessary in this case, since the framework is used as part of the learning process, it is important to note that students should be given the option not to take part in an activity if they do not wish to do so. My experience is that it is uncommon to find students who do not want to express their views; on the contrary, they like the idea of having their views heard. This also relates to the issue of students being given the choice of keeping their views anonymous or not. This has implications when analysing the information gathered and I will come back to this issue through the description of specific activities.

What is very important and ethically essential is for students to know the ways in which the information that will be gained from them will be used. In particular: Who will look at the information? Will it be shared in some form with others? These questions relate to confidentiality, which has to be clearly explained to the students from the beginning. The confidentiality issue is one that might affect students' responses and therefore is one that has to be treated with great care. This issue of confidentiality is one that is discussed in more detail later in this chapter, since it is of crucial importance and relates to some of the decisions that teachers have to make in order to move forward.

Who should facilitate the process?

As already discussed in Chapters 1 and 2, using the framework involves a collaborative process, in which both members of staff and students are seen as making equally important contributions, and both can learn through participating. However, there is definitely a need for someone, or a group of people, to facilitate the whole process. This could be either adults or even students, especially in secondary schools.

In some contexts, as for example in countries where support staff are not appointed in schools, reference to adults would only mean teachers. In one such example of a primary school, even the headteacher volunteered to carry out some of the activities, in addition to the teachers collecting data, since she was very interested in finding out what the students felt about their experiences in her school. She also led the whole process.

In this particular context, the headteacher had teaching responsibilities and incorporated some of the activities into her own teaching practices. The teachers also incorporated the activities into their own teaching, but the one who kept the whole process going was the headteacher. However, this might not be applicable in contexts where headteachers do not have teaching responsibilities. Of course, all of this is challenging in terms of the time available for a headteacher to be engaged in such a process. The fact that the headteacher was leading the process, and, most importantly, the fact that it was a whole school approach, had a significant impact on the outcomes of the project.

In English schools, where there is generally speaking a wealth of support staff, they often have a key role in facilitating the process. So, for example, in one school with which I worked, two learning mentors took the role of the facilitators. Learning mentors are salaried members of staff who work with students, usually combining academic and pastoral support roles with the aim of ensuring that students engage more effectively in learning and achieve appropriately (http://www.cwdcouncil.org.uk/learning-mentors/). In other schools, this role was given to teaching assistants, whereas in other contexts it was teachers themselves who led the whole process. As I have indicated, in schools where senior staff are prepared to be more daring, assigning the roles of co-researchers to students puts them in the leading role. However, even in such cases in most examples an assigned adult or two were also supporting the students in the process. What is very important is that if students are chosen to act as co-researchers they should receive some form of training about how to use the framework and various methods of data collection and analysis.

When should the framework be used and for how long?

Another question that teachers may be thinking about is when to use the framework and for how long. Again there is not a single answer to this and schools have chosen to approach this differently according to their individual timetables.

The issue of time is of great importance and should not be underestimated. For the first step, teachers can use many of the activities within their daily lessons. However, for the second step of the framework, practitioners need to set some time aside to look at the information and where possible in collaboration with others. In some contexts, this time might be available; for example, when teachers have allocated periods of the day for joint planning; in some contexts this might not be possible, however, and teachers might have to be released from other duties to get together. These issues are context specific and are likely to be dealt with as they emerge. What is of importance, though, is that time should be set aside in order to engage meaningfully with the information gathered.

What are the ethical considerations that need to be kept in mind?

Research with children and its importance have been extensively discussed in the literature (e.g. Ainscow and Kaplan, 2005; Carrington *et al.*, 2010; Fielding, 2001; Thomson, 2010). In what follows, I provide a summary of the issues that need to be taken into account when carrying out research with children and young people, since the central focus of the framework is on students' voices. Emphasis will be given to ethical dimensions of doing research with children and young people; however, ethics, as we have already seen, is a theme that pervades the whole process of using the framework. It is also discussed more specifically in Chapter 5, when the issue of sharing data with other practitioners and students is explored in greater detail.

Mayall (2001) refers to two approaches when carrying out research that involves children. According to her, the first one accepts the generational order meaning that the adult is superior to the child, and has the knowledge to document childhood in the light of that knowledge. In other words, this can be described as 'research on children'. On the other hand, the second approach questions this generational order and emphasises the fact that good information about childhood must start from children themselves, and therefore this kind of research can be named 'research with children'. She argues, though, that children do see adults as having power over them. I certainly agree with this point and I also argue that, especially in school contexts, these power relationships between adults and children and young people are more apparent.

Morrow and Richards (1996) suggest that the biggest ethical challenge for researchers who involve children in their research is the disparities in power and status between adults and children. They argue that

> using methods which are non-invasive, non confrontational and participatory, and which encourage children to interpret their own data, might be one step forward in diminishing the ethical problems of imbalanced relationships between researcher and researched at the point of data collection and interpretation.
>
> (p. 100)

Taking into consideration these points, the framework involves techniques and methods that are non-invasive, non-confrontational and participatory to the greatest possible extent. These are described in the following chapter. At the same time, the suggested techniques are constructive, in the sense that they are intended to bring to the surface the individual's viewpoint. Also, Step 3 of the framework allows children to interpret their own data; therefore, this is another way to address issues of disparities in power between adults and students.

In essence, using an approach of the sort I am suggesting through the framework, whereby teachers and students take the roles of collaborators, it is essential for adults to operate in such ways and to use such methods that could reduce the barriers that already exist on account of these power relationships. As a consequence, the impact of power relationships is likely to be reduced.

This issue of power relationships also relates to a whole range of other ethical issues when doing research with students. Beginning with the issue of gaining consent to do research with children, as Thomas and O'Kane (1998) argue, this is complicated by the fact that both adults' and children's consent is required. In reality, unless you have the adults' consent, particularly that of the parents, then you cannot move on to request children's consent. In this sense, children's choice to participate or not in research is limited.

Thomas and O'Kane go on to argue that another ethical issue, which is more problematic in research with children, is that of confidentiality, since there may be adults who expect to be told about children's thoughts for whom they are responsible. I certainly ended up in this situation in some schools, where teachers were expecting me to tell them what the students said in their interviews. Of course, as researchers, we do know that we cannot, and should not, breach confidentiality in any case.

As I have explained, the framework can be used by practitioners in schools, or by researchers, or by students working as co-researchers. Different levels of ethical considerations are relevant in each case. For example, the idea of teachers using the framework as part of their daily work does not usually require ethical permissions from parents. This is what schools did where teachers used the framework as part of their work, as I discussed before. On the contrary, where I used the framework as a researcher, ethical permissions from parents and students were gained. Similarly, where the framework was used as part of a research project, as for example in secondary schools where students were acting as co-researchers, they gained consent from their classmates that they were happy to participate in the project. In addition, ethical issues for dealing with information gained through the use of the framework are still there to be dealt with in any case, and these will be discussed in greater detail in the following chapters.

Summary and conclusion

This chapter provided one example of a primary school that used the framework as a way of engaging with students' voices in order to improve its practices. In addition, generic guidance regarding specific issues that relate to the use of the framework in schools was provided, based on experience gained through using the framework in a number of contexts. As seen through the example, each individual context and its participants will shape the process suggested by the framework and this has to be kept in mind at all times. In the example, teachers led the process; however, collaboration with students and collaboration with other practitioners was crucial in implementing the framework. The next chapter deals with the details of the first step of the framework. Illustrative examples from a number of schools are provided.

Chapter 3

Opening doors

Enabling voices to emerge

In this chapter a range of practical approaches for identifying issues related to marginalisation are described. Ethical considerations related to the use of these approaches with children and young people about such sensitive issues are also discussed. The emphasis throughout is on finding ways of engaging with children's and young people's voices, and different methods and techniques that can be used in order to bring to the surface views of pupils are presented. In addition, illustrative examples of the use of these techniques are provided.

'Opening doors'

Researching marginalisation is by no means an easy process. As discussed in the previous chapter, marginalisation is a complex and, at times, elusive concept. Based on the typology that emerged through my earlier work, it is clear that what counts as marginalisation for some may not be perceived as such by those who appear to experience it. The elusiveness of the term therefore makes it complicated to research. In addition, understanding marginalisation, especially from children's and young people's perspectives, is such a sensitive area that special caution should be taken in order to carry out research that is ethically acceptable. Consequently, it is essential to keep in mind the ethical issues discussed in the previous chapter at all times, not least in order to consider the ways in which power relationships can be minimised through the use of the methods and techniques described in this chapter.

Some authors (e.g. Fraser, 2004; Punch, 2002a) argue that research with children is different from research with adults, not least because of the power relationships that exist between adults and children and young people that I mentioned in the previous chapter. Christensen and James (2001), however, argue that research with children does not necessarily entail adapting different methods, although some techniques may be more appropriate to use with children. This is a view that I also endorse. That is why in the title of the first step of the framework I use the metaphor 'opening doors'. In other words, by using specific methods and techniques we are aiming at enabling students to express their views, and allow marginalised voices to come to the surface, as well as issues that are of concern.

In referring to his band, The Doors, the singer Jim Morrison said: 'There are things known and things unknown. And in between are the doors' (Sugerman, 2001, back cover). In essence, I view these methods and techniques as the ones opening the doors that will enable us to uncover subtle issues that we are not familiar with. Consequently, by doing this we may move into unknown territories, or view known ones in a new light.

All the methods and techniques described here are intended to be used as part of the first step of the framework. In what follows I offer advice on using them, based on my experience. Some of the methods and techniques are adaptations of ones that have been described in other sources for different purposes. These adaptations have been made in order to fit the area under investigation: that of marginalisation. Some others have been developed in collaboration with practitioners and students in primary and secondary schools. Each method and technique is discussed in detail, and reference to ethical issues is also made, where necessary.

Readers will understand that some methods and techniques are relatively straightforward to use, whereas others are more complicated and time-consuming. However, those involved must judge which are more appropriate, based on what they want to find out, and taking account of the school context and the flexibility that they have within that context.

The suggested approaches are aimed at both primary as well as secondary schools. Some of these can also be used in early years settings. The list is not exhaustive. Rather, it is indicative of the types of methods and techniques that I have found useful. It also reveals the creativity that has been exhibited by both teachers and students in developing further activities.

As I present the methods and techniques, I address issues that need to be taken into account when using them, whether this involves teachers, students, researchers, or some combination of these. Clearly, there are some issues that relate to implementing the method and technique in general, regardless of who is involved. However, there are some issues that relate only to teachers and these will be highlighted as each method and technique is described.

Ways of 'opening doors'

In what follows, the different methods and techniques that have been found useful as ways of 'opening doors' for students are presented. First, the two overall methods that are widely used in social sciences research with students are described: observations and interviews. Later, I present a number of other ways that can be used in research with students that facilitate an engagement with students' voices and that I have used in my work with schools. As I point out, such approaches can be used by themselves, or as part of interviews too, in order to facilitate conversations with students.

Observation

Teachers observe naturally in their daily work but many times these observations are not carried out in a systematic way, or with a given focus. The role of observation is central within early years provision, especially in England, and there is plenty of useful literature around it (e.g. Hobart and Frankel, 2004; Riddall-Leech, 2005; Sharman *et al.*, 2003; Smidt, 2005). Unfortunately, as students grow older, and go into primary and secondary schools, not so much importance is given to systematic observation. Of course, this is because of the heavy timetables of primary and secondary schools; however, even unplanned observations can generate useful information for those teachers who wish to engage with students' voices and reactions to what is happening in schools.

To take an example, one primary school that used the framework found that its incidental observations led to discussions about individual students during a staff meeting. Teachers, through these unplanned observations, identified students who they felt might experience marginalisation, and therefore decided to start observing more closely their behaviours in various lessons and in the wider school settings. So, whenever an incident had occurred that seemed to be interesting, teachers made brief notes summarising what had happened in order to look at it more closely later on. In this simple way, observations enable practitioners to stop and think about what was happening in classrooms and schools. In addition, it enables teachers to become more reflective about their own actions and the impact they have on students. This relates to Schon's (1987) idea about what characterises highly skilled practitioners within the professions: that is, the capacity to analyse situations and use their expertise drawn from prior experience to invent appropriate responses. As Schon defines it, this process involves reflection-in-action, as experienced practitioners improvise. He also proposes that, for purposes of professional development, opportunities to reflect-on-action can be very helpful. So, for example, in a situation of the sort I have just described we saw how teachers used observations in order to reflect-on-action.

The focus in this section is on purposeful observation and how it can be used as part of the framework. In general terms there are two different kinds of observation: quantitative and qualitative (Wragg, 2000). The quantitative approach may involve different types of rating scales, the use of time-sampling techniques, or various forms of structured observations. Qualitative observations usually involve open, exploratory methods, although sometimes more focused forms of observation, such as the monitoring of critical events may be adopted (see Wragg, 2000, for detailed suggestions in regard to all these approaches).

Here, I choose to focus only on open and structured observations, as these were found to be most relevant in schools that I worked with. When using open observations the observer tries to capture anything significant that is observed by keeping detailed notes (Hopkins, 2008). On the other hand, structured observations are more focused, using predetermined categories or indicators against which the observer has to record whether something is happening or not, or keep a tally every time an example is noted. Examples of each of these kinds of observations are provided later in the chapter.

Hopkins (2008) defines four key features of classroom observation: joint planning, focus, establishing criteria, and observation skills and feedback. He mainly refers to peer observation, where teachers observe their colleagues, or in some instances, where students observe teachers. It has to be made clear here that for the purposes of the framework the emphasis is usually on teachers observing students, and in some cases, where students acted as co-researchers, students observing lessons. Of course, in settings where timetable flexibility allowed, peer observations among colleagues were also carried out. However, since the focus of this framework is on marginalisation, and in essence who is left out of learning and social processes in schools, observations were mainly focusing on students in the class, or outside in the playground. Nevertheless, what students do in class is certainly related to how the teachers organise their lessons.

Regarding open observations, practitioners should be clear about the fact that what they write down is simply what they observe, and not their personal thoughts or interpretations about the observations. This is something that has to follow in the next step of the framework, when looking closely at the information gathered. Consequently, the notes should be brief, explaining clearly what has occurred.

An example of an observation that a teacher noted down after she finished the lesson is provided in Figure 3.1. (NB: Use is made of the third person singular – instead of first person – since such observation notes were to be shared with others during steps 2 and 3 of the framework.)

The fact that no comments or personal interpretations should be made on the observations notes is something that teachers struggle with. This relates to what Hopkins (2008) describes as one of the observation skills that are essential for successful classroom observation: that practitioners should be 'guarding against the natural tendency to move too quickly into judgement' (p. 77). Even though this point is crucial, teachers – or student co-researchers – do

---

The teacher is asking students to find the meaning of words in the dictionary. Then they discuss these words and have to write sentences. After they have discussed these words, Hilary puts up her hand and says: 'Miss, what does "trophy" mean?' (one of the words that they explained a while ago). Everyone else starts laughing. Hilary blushes and has a sad expression on her face.

Figure 3.1 An extract from a teacher's observation notes.

not have the luxury of time to devote to analysing observations, as researchers do. Therefore, I suggest a midway approach, which involves a second column next to the observations, where comments, thoughts and interpretations can be noted at the time that observations are made (see, for example, Figure 3.2 which relates to the observation notes in Figure 3.1) or a little later. Then, during the second step, practitioners can add more comments in that column that they would like to explore further.

Open observations can be used within any context and are a powerful means for thinking about what is experienced by students. It can be potentially powerful amongst those students who have communication difficulties, particularly in trying to experience school activities from the point of view of the students. For example, in a special school that I worked with, for students in the age range 11–19 years who experienced severe and profound learning difficulties, observation was used as a way of collecting the views of pupils about the curriculum, teaching and learning. Given the complex nature of the difficulties of some of the students and communication difficulties with those students, observation was used as the sole method to explore their experiences. Staff observed their colleagues' lessons, focusing on individual students. They tried to see the lesson through the eyes of particular pupils, in order to determine the extent to which the content and activities were meaningful and relevant. The class teacher decided in advance which pupils she would like the observer to focus on. In some cases the member of staff observing did not know much about the chosen pupil before hand and would get some background information from their colleagues before actually watching the lesson.

Noting the impact that this programme of observations had on staff attitudes and thinking, the head commented:

Observation notes	Comments
The teacher is asking students to find the meaning of words in the dictionary. Then they discuss these words and have to write sentences. After they have discussed these words, Hilary puts up her hand and says: 'Miss, what does "trophy" mean?' (one of the words that they explained a while ago). Everyone else starts laughing. Hilary blushes and has a sad expression on her face.	Does she do this to get attention? Did she really not hear when it was explained? I need to make sure that I always have her attention when explaining. How does she feel now that everyone is laughing? Would they laugh if the same question were asked by a 'good' student? How can we make others respect their classmates' questions – even if they sound funny to them?

Figure 3.2 Observation notes with teacher's comments.

I loved it. Sit back and watch for an hour and half and watch what a child was telling us – I really enjoyed it. It was really interesting. Not just being an advocate, actually trying to understand what the children are saying to us. It helped us unpick ways . . . to be more thoughtful on how to ask questions.

Her view was that this kind of observation had provided a powerful tool for staff development. More specifically, it had, she argued, served as a platform for further reflection on current ways of working, whilst, at the same time, provoking them to think how these practices were experienced by the pupils.

In another secondary school, students who worked as co-researchers developed a set of questions/areas that they wanted to focus on when they were observing lessons. In particular they focused on the areas in Figure 3.3.

Therefore, the students were using rather focused open observations. In other words, they had these areas that they wanted to focus on but they kept descriptive notes on what they were observing. It has to be noted here that, in those cases where students carried out observations in schools, they had to receive training in order to be in a position to do this. In Figure 3.4 some generic guidelines that were given to students can be found.

In other schools, use was made of more systematic observation strategies. The schedule in Figure 3.5 is one such example.

We have used this schedule in both primary and secondary schools. In particular, when using it we focused on identifying whether some students were

---

- Does anyone seem left out?
- Participation
- Friendship groups
- Does anyone look lost or unwilling?
- Other comments

Figure 3.3 Students' areas of focus while observing lessons.

Make sure that:

- people know in advance that you will be observing in their class
- you do not interrupt the lesson in any way
- you write down what you observe – see and hear – and not what you think about what you are observing
- you do not mention anyone's names.

Figure 3.4 Guidelines for students who carry out observations.

Observation schedule

Date:
Lesson:

Please circle one.   Please note 1= low, 4=high

Students work independently	1	2	3	4
Students ask questions relevant to the lesson	1	2	3	4
Students listen to each other	1	2	3	4
Students respect other peoples' views	1	2	3	4
Students work collaboratively in the lesson	1	2	3	4
Students participate in the lesson	1	2	3	4
Students seem to enjoy the lesson	1	2	3	4
There are students that seem disengaged	1	2	3	4
There are students who struggle	1	2	3	4
There are students who do not express their views	1	2	3	4
There are students who sit on their own	1	2	3	4

Any other comments:

Figure 3.5 An observation schedule.

marginalised within a classroom context. By focusing directly on participation, students who are marginalised in a classroom context can be identified. Like other authors, I feel that using a fragmented predetermined set of categories in systematic classroom observations prevents recognition of the complexity of classroom behaviour (see, for example, Delamont and Hamilton, 1993; Walker and Adelman, 1993). As McIntyre and Macleod (1993) argue, one of the criticisms when using systematic classroom observations is that links and chains of behaviour are lost, which from my point of view might be as important as the behaviours themselves. However, practitioners seem to find systematic observations easy to use as well as time efficient.

If possible, it is better if such observation schedules are used at the same time by two people. Then a comparison can be made. Where we did this it led to fruitful discussions among observers. Furthermore, it highlighted further the fact that, even though it may appear easy to fill in such schedules, it is very likely that there will be differences in the ratings that individual observers give for the observation statements. Therefore, this leads to useful discussions and further reflections about what is happening in classrooms.

Of course, it is clear that such approaches require peer observation by a colleague, or even by one of the students. Some teachers chose to be observed by someone when they were teaching their own classes, whereas others chose to observe someone else teaching their own class or year group. Ideally, both should be used and could provide insightful information.

Peer observation is an invaluable method for teachers' professional development and in many contexts is used in effective and constructive ways. I am aware, though, that in many schools peer observation is not a common practice and teachers might find this process threatening. What needs to be made clear here is that for the purposes of using this framework the focus is on students' participation in the class. Of course, students' engagement and participation within a lesson is inextricably linked to the actions and behaviours of the teachers, as was mentioned earlier. Nevertheless, I do believe that teachers who choose to engage with the framework are willing to be challenged about their own practices and listen to what their colleagues have to say, as well as to what the students have to say. In addition, peer observation should not only be seen as a way of identifying weaknesses but, equally, as a way of identifying strengths too.

In summary, then, there are different kinds of observations and here I have focused on the two that are most relevant when using the framework: open and systematic observations. Further useful examples can be found in Hopkins's (2008) book, where various other kinds of observations that teachers can use in the classroom are explained.

What I would like to stress here is that observation as a method is particularly helpful in the way it can provide an opportunity to reflect on what is on offer in a given context. Unless we are given that opportunity to sit back and observe what is happening in a classroom context, simple things that can have an important impact on student participation can so easily be ignored. I would add that observation techniques can be and, wherever possible, should be combined with other approaches, not least that of interviews.

Interviews

Interviews have been defined as a conversation with a purpose (Robson, 1993). They can take different forms: structured, semi-structured or unstructured.

Interviews provide us with a means of exploring the points of view of research participants (Miller and Glassner, 1997) and allow for greater depth than questionnaires (Cohen and Manion, 1994). For the purposes of the framework, those who take the roles of interviewees are most often the students and they may be interviewed either by adults or by other classmates.

Interviews are time-consuming. However, the richness of data that they can provide us with is invaluable. This means that using interviews as part of the framework process is quite demanding but definitely worthwhile.

One of the first decisions that need to be made is whether to carry out interviews with groups, with pairs of pupils or with individuals. There is no doubt that group interviews are less time-consuming than those with individuals. However, there is always the danger that during a group discussion one person might dominate the process, and therefore act as a barrier for individual expression (Dockrell et al., 2000; Fontana and Frey, 1998; Watts and Ebbutt, 1987). On the other hand, it is possible that the presence of a group of children might help reluctant individuals to talk, but I would say that this very much depends on the children that are in the group and the relations between them, as well as the area being discussed. Therefore, it is quite crucial to decide on what our focus will be for the interviews.

When exploring general issues about school life that have been brought up through the use of other techniques, it might well be appropriate to use group interviews. In such contexts the presence of a group of children can be helpful in order that those involved can bounce ideas off one another. However, where more sensitive issues are involved that concern individuals, then it might not be easy for these to be discussed within a group setting.

Illustrating the point, Punch (2002b) used both group and individual interviews in her research with young people, aged thirteen to fourteen, from mainstream schools and residential care units. Her work explored young people's perceptions of their problems, their coping strategies and their help-seeking behaviour. It was interesting that at the end of the research she asked youngsters to say which kind of interviews they liked and why. Though there were differences in the sample in terms of gender and place of residence, nearly three quarters of the mainstream school sample preferred the group interviews, whereas two thirds of the residential school group preferred individual interviews. Those who preferred the individual interviews, from any of the samples, felt that they were more confidential, more private and more 'about you'. Those who were in favour of the group interviews said that they were more humorous and it was easier to talk with friends. In this sense, it can be argued that individual interviews are more appropriate for exploring sensitive issues such as issues related to marginalisation. In the light of her experiences, Punch offers the helpful suggestion that young people should be given the choice to be interviewed in a group, individually or with a friend of their choice.

The idea of interviewing children in pairs, when children pick a friend to have an interview with, is also suggested by Mayall (2001) and is another option to consider. In my own study on understanding marginalisation this idea was rejected since it was not thought to be appropriate because of the area of investigation (Messiou, 2003). My feeling was that it would not be appropriate to ask children to speak in front of others about who might not have any friends, or who might not feel comfortable with other children. There was also the possibility that some children might not be chosen by anyone and this would possibly upset them. I therefore decided that such a sensitive issue as marginalisation would be better investigated through individual interviews. However, as I have suggested, given the time constraints of practitioners in busy schools this could be given as an option to students and then the ones who wanted to be interviewed individually would be in a position to choose.

Who is carrying out the interview is another important decision. Of all the activities that are described here, given the face-to-face nature of the interviews, it is perhaps often better for someone other than practitioners to carry out the interviews. As I found out, where it is possible, an external researcher can be an ideal person to carry out interviews in schools, since it is likely that students will open up more to an outsider than an insider (Messiou and Jones, 2011). Some schools have even used parents to interview groups of students, although in such cases special consideration should be given to the importance of avoiding discussions about individual teachers or students. Furthermore, students were ideal choices in those schools where we worked with them as co-researchers, especially when students from a specific year group interviewed students from a different year group. Having students as interviewers might also be one way of minimising the adult–student power relationships that were discussed earlier. More importantly, we felt that students who were interviewed by students felt very comfortable talking to them. Of course, as with observations, students who are going to act as interviewers need to receive training about how to carry out successful interviews and how to address ethical issues. The generic guidelines in Figure 3.6 were provided in such sessions, even though the most important aspect of such training sessions is letting the students experience what it feels like being interviewed. Through this experimentation they are likely to develop the necessary skills for interviewing.

Make sure that:

- people are happy to be interviewed by you
- you are friendly with the people you interview and respect their answers
- you have prepared a set of questions in advance to help you during the interview
- you avoid questions that can give only yes or no answers.

Figure 3.6 General guidelines for students who carry out interviews.

Another important decision that has to be made concerns the format of the interviews used with children. Given the fact that the focus is on marginalisation, and all the potential sensitivities this may imply, there is a big challenge in finding ways of getting children to talk in a comfortable way. Certainly I would not ask children and young people directly whether or not they experience marginalisation. First of all the term in itself is very difficult, but more importantly for ethical reasons this is not an issue to be directly addressed. Furthermore, students who might experience marginalisation might not feel very comfortable about discussing it. Such concerns can be addressed through the use of specific techniques.

Harden and colleagues (2000) argue that the need to create special techniques in order to interview children is premised on the belief that this is more difficult than talking to adults; in this way they construct children as 'other' in methodological terms. I would like to point out that this is not the assumption underlying the suggestion of such techniques in my work. Instead, the effort to approach indirectly a sensitive issue – marginalisation – led to the need to find special techniques, and not the assumption that children are somehow inferior to adults. I would also argue that the same principles of interviewing apply to both adults and children and young people, as for example asking open-ended questions, using probes and avoiding leading questions (Robson, 1993). However, certain techniques can be useful for elicitation purposes, and some of these are more appropriate for use with children rather than with adults. Having said that, I have used such techniques for interviewing adults (e.g. Messiou, in preparation). In particular, I have used scenarios as part of the interview process both with adults and with children of primary school age. Of course, different scenarios were used and in each case they were adapted for the purposes of each interview, but the technique was more or less the same.

In the literature, there is a vast number of suggested techniques to use when doing research with children, and especially when interviewing (e.g. Davies, 2000; Davis, 2000; Hall and McGregor, 2000; Hazel, 1995; Lewis, 1995, 2002; Mauthner, 1997; O'Kane, 2000; Punch, 2002b; Thomas and O'Kane, 1998; Vlachou, 1997). Among the techniques suggested are the use of drawings; using images, such as pictures, photographs and cue cards; using games; and storytelling. The aim of such techniques is to facilitate children's talking and to make the discussions more enjoyable. More about techniques that can be used in interviews with children is discussed later on in this chapter.

In summary, then, the key thing in using interviews to elicit the views of children and young people is to find ways to encourage them talk, without making them feel uncomfortable in any way. This is where the use of the various techniques discussed later in this chapter is likely to be useful in eliciting views in a non-threatening way. In this effort to approach sensitive issues indirectly I have found the need to adopt such special techniques. As I have stressed, this does not mean that children and young people are viewed as somehow inferior to adults and as people who would not open up in an interview situation; it is rather the topic itself that provides the necessity to use other techniques to address the issue indirectly. In addition, as I will illustrate, such techniques can make the interview more enjoyable.

Facilitating conversations with students

In this section, a number of ways that have been used in order to facilitate conversations with students are explored. In choosing the particular methods and techniques I have favoured those that allow students to express their own views without being influenced by the presence of an adult, and that help in creating a pleasant and supportive atmosphere. I have found them to be particularly useful in gaining students' interest and helping them to feel comfortable. As I will explain, some of the methods can be used as part of an interview, in a whole class situation, or with groups of students. It is important to keep in mind that how these approaches are used is only suggested. Therefore, putting any of these methods in these broad categories should be seen as a loose pattern that allows for flexibility.

Working with groups of students or in an interview situation

The methods that follow can be used as part of interviews, as well as on their own within whole class sessions. I choose to present them here while the readers have fresh in their minds issues that are related to interviews.

Message in a bottle

This is a technique used by Davies (2000) to investigate children's understanding of democratic processes in primary schools. I used the idea for my first study on marginalisation as an indirect way of identifying students who might possibly experience marginalisation (Messiou, 2003). I have also used the technique during individual interviews with children.

Message in a bottle can be used on its own by practitioners, or students as co-researchers, for the purposes of using the framework. Students are asked to write, or speak, a message that would be sent to another planet, stating something that they are not happy with at school and would like to change. The aim is to bring to the surface possible examples of marginalisation.

I have found that the activity enables children and young people to express their views in a non-threatening way. The technique can be used in a number of different ways. For example, where I used this technique as part of individual interviews with students I had the flexibility to give them the choice to either say or write down their message, taking into account the differences among children and the fact that some of the children might have difficulties with writing. In the interview process this worked well and many children showed relief when they were given the option of saying instead of writing the message. On the other hand, where practitioners in schools used this activity, it was used in situations where all students were gathered as a class, or in a group. Therefore, giving this option of writing or saying the message was not possible. Certainly this might present difficulties for some particular children and young people who might struggle with writing.

Confidentiality and anonymity is another issue that should be thought about. If the activity is anonymous, then there is a danger of not being in a position to identify the concerns of particular students and, therefore, act on them. On the other hand, if students know that they can be identified they might not freely express their views. That is why confidentiality is so important with this activity and the researcher must clarify it and ensure students' understanding of it at the beginning of the activity. In other words, students should be given the option of identifying who they are or not and should be assured that, if they decide to disclose their identity, whatever they say will remain confidential.

Sociometric measures

An approach which explores relationships among members of a group is social network analysis. Wasserman and Faust (1994) explain that:

> The phrase 'social network' refers to the set of actors and the ties among them. The network analyst would seek to model these relationships to depict the structure of a group. One could then study the impact of this structure on the functioning of the group and/or the influence of this structure on individuals within the group.
>
> (p. 9)

One of the pioneers of social network analysis was Moreno (1934), who developed the sociogram technique. Sociograms are visual representations of the relationships between all the people of a particular group. Specifically, in a sociogram people are represented as points and the relationships between them as arrows (see example in Figure 3.7).

However, according to Moreno, the sociogram is not just the visual representation of the responses of the participants but first of all is a method for exploration. This will be discussed further in the following chapter.

For the purposes of using the framework, students are asked to nominate three children they would like to play with and three they would like to work with, if they could choose. In this way, we can identify the least and most liked students within a given context. It should be noted that it is very important to ask students to make only positive nominations, rather than asking students to think in negative ways about their classmates, especially since the framework aims to promote inclusion.

Then these nominations are presented visually, in order that they can be further analysed in the next step of the framework. In my work with schools

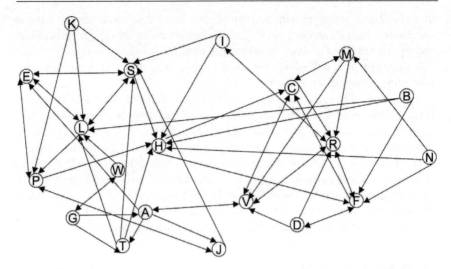

Figure 3.7 A sociogram.

I found that it is easier for teachers to chart students' nominations on a table – the approach used in the school in Chapter 2 – rather than develop an actual sociogram. In this way, teachers can easily highlight the most favoured and least favoured students during the next step of the framework. How sociometric measures can be analysed, and follow-up activities as a means of validation and further exploration, are described in the next chapter.

Sociometric measures can also be used as part of individual interviews with students, where the activity can move beyond the simple nomination by asking them to justify their choices. For example, instead of just having a set of questions to explore during an interview, sociometric measures could be used for the opening of a conversation. The power of using sociometric measures in individual interviews rather than with a whole group is that, first, it provides us with an opportunity to identify the least liked students according to students' views, and, second, it can be used as an indirect way to ask about other students. In this way, an exploration of children's attitudes towards specific classmates can be made. Particularly, students are asked not only to name three classmates they would like to play with and three they would like to work with but to give the reasons they would choose these. In this way, a further exploration on the reasons students choose particular pupils, either as their favourites or as their least favourites, can be made. In other words, even though the nominations that students are asked to make are positive, it did happen to me that when students were justifying those choices they referred to other students who were not popular. For example, one student said to me 'I would choose Mary because she is well-behaved and very kind. She is not like Helen, for example, who always creates problems'. Helen was one in the specific class who was not nominated by anyone, and therefore this other student provided me with some reasons why she was not popular. Therefore, if sociometric measures are used as part of an interview they can provide us with such additional information that can be further explored in the next step of the framework.

Visual images

Recently, the use of visual images has become popular when engaging with students' voices. There is plenty of literature regarding such approaches and the benefits as well as the complexities of using them with children and young people (e.g. Burke, 2008; Kaplan, 2008; Kaplan and Howes, 2004; Thomson, 2008b). Thomson (2008a) distinguishes between two ways in which social scientists approach the visual. As she argues, the first approach is when researchers take visual artefacts and explore how these were produced and their uses as well as how participants interpret them, whereas the second approach refers to the production of visual artefacts as part of the research process.

The examples that I am referring to here relate mainly to the second approach. Specifically, I refer to the use of drawings, the photo voice technique and the use of videos for carrying out research with students.

Drawings are a relatively easy method to use. They can be used as an elicitation technique at the beginning of interviews, or they can be used within a whole group situation. Since the focus here is on marginalisation, what we did in schools was that we asked students to draw something that happened at school that made them upset, or something that was happening in school that they were unhappy with. Two examples are provided in Figures 3.8 and 3.9.

In Figure 3.8 a girl drew herself crying because a boy told her that she was black and made fun of her. This girl was from a mixed-race marriage and in that particular school the majority of the children were white. As she explained, making fun of her skin colour was something that often happened. The drawing in Figure 3.9 was produced by a boy who wanted to show how the others never played with him, and that this made him very sad and he cried. Thus, using the drawings at the start of the interview in these cases enabled me to start the conversations in a relaxed and natural way. It also facilitated discussion about sensitive issues in an indirect way. Drawings can also be used with whole groups of students, with the observer keeping notes about what students say as they draw.

Photo voice activities were widely used amongst the schools that I have worked with. It has been defined as a 'participatory action research strategy by which people create and discuss photographs as a means of catalysing personal and community change' (Wang et al., 1998). In my work, both practitioners and students have been very positive about photo voice and have commented that it is very popular among students. However, in order for the technique to be effective and result in meaningful data, a number of issues have to be thought about.

First of all, it has to be decided if students will work individually, in pairs or in groups. In the schools that I worked with, most of the times the staff

Figure 3.8 A drawing by a girl.

Figure 3.9 A drawing by a boy.

invited students to work in small groups, usually threes or pairs. This was to ensure that all the students had a chance to use the camera and also to save time. This approach has limitations as well as advantages. For example, it does allow students to discuss and come up with a decision about what they will show in the picture; therefore, they have to agree on what they are taking pictures of. Moreover, through this process of dialogue among students it is likely that they will reflect further on what they experience in schools. The dilemmas associated with this technique when it is used by groups or pairs relate to whose view is depicted in the pictures. Specifically, is it one person's view or a shared view? Again, ideally if someone can follow students and write down the conversations that are taking place while the students discuss to decide what to include in these pictures, this will generate information that could be used later on for the purpose of analysis.

The general guidelines in Figure 3.10 have proved to be useful for students before they start taking pictures. Similar issues apply when students are asked to produce videos. Clearly, students need to receive training about filming and they need to be given clear instructions about the duration of the film they will produce, otherwise they might end up with overlong films. In schools that we worked with we found that using the cameras is not so difficult, given the technology facilities available and the students' familiarity with these. However, issues similar to the ones mentioned in Figure 3.10 have to be discussed in advance.

In one school, children were put into pairs and, with the use of flip cameras (small cameras the size of a mobile phone which digitally record high-definition videos), had to film what they felt helped them to learn in the class and what made it difficult for them. Issues of consent were also addressed here. Specifically, those who did not want to be filmed were identified so that they would not appear. In fact, only one student did not want his face shown in the films. Each pair had the flip camera for a day and then they had to present to their class what they filmed.

Very useful guidance regarding the practicalities and details of using the visual images approach can be found in Kaplan (2008). The products of the

---

Make sure that you:

- respect when people tell you they do not want to be shown in pictures
- discuss with your partners before taking a picture
- are clear about what you want to show through the picture you are taking
- limit the number of pictures you take.

Figure 3.10 Guidelines for students using the photo voice approach.

visual images approach can be also be used as a way of facilitating conversations with students in interviews situations. In addition, they can be used in the third step of the framework for further analysis and understandings of what is happening in the schools. One such example is provided in Chapter 5.

Working with groups of students

The methods and techniques that follow are mainly used with groups of students, or even whole classes, usually within the classroom. This does not mean that it takes away the flexibility from teachers to use these as they feel is most appropriate. However, my experience has demonstrated that usually they are best used with groups. Often, too, their use is followed by some form of interview in order to explore in more detail issues that have been brought up.

Circle time

This activity is extensively used in English schools. It is aimed at developing participants' awareness of themselves and of others (Canney and Byrne, 2006). During circle time activities, students sit in a circle and take turns to complete a sentence that the teacher has started. For example, 'I like my friend X because she/he is . . .' However, for the purposes of the use of the framework, circle time activities can be used as a way of identifying what the students like in their schools or in their classrooms. So, the sentence could be 'In my school I like . . . because . . .' or 'I am good at . . .'.

It is best that students are asked to use only positive statements, since everyone can hear what one another is saying. Indeed, in some English schools circle time is used at the beginning or towards the end of the school day, precisely for this reason – to start or finish with positive thinking.

The statements that the students will complete are not directly related to marginalisation as such. However, by listening to what they value in schools helps practitioners in thinking about how to organise learning in such ways so as to be more inclusive. Alternatively, practitioners might listen to things that they have never thought of before. For example, I remember once in a primary school a little girl said, 'I am not good at anything.' Up to that time the teacher did not really think that the girl felt like that, even though she did know that the girl was lacking in confidence. Examples like this remind us that students' statements can sometimes be revealing for practitioners. In addition, they may prove to be helpful in terms of organising experiences that will enable students to feel more confident and be successful at the same time.

It should be noted that, in school contexts where circle time is not a common practice, careful planning has to be made in advance and rules have to be agreed with students. For example, it has to be made clear to students that they have to listen to one another and wait for each person to finish what they are saying and most importantly respect one another's ideas. Laughing at people's views should not be allowed, nor disrespecting anyone's view in any way.

The feelings dice

This is based on an activity originally suggested by McNamara and Moreton (1995). As the title implies, the aim is to explore feelings. Children are given a die that they have to throw and, according to which side is showing, complete statements such as 'I am happy when . . .'/'I am sad when . . .' (Figure 3.11). Usually the outcomes of this technique are similar to those generated through circle time. However, the process seems to work well in engaging individuals, especially for primary school children.

It is important to note that, with these two activities (circle time and feelings die), ideally someone should be observing and keeping notes of the students' comments, especially those that might be of concern. In this way there is a record of what the students have said in order to analyse that information further in the next step. However, sometimes this may not be possible. For example, in contexts where only one teacher is able to be present when such activities are taking place, it is up to that individual practitioner to take brief notes at the end the activity in order to have some information to look at during the next step.

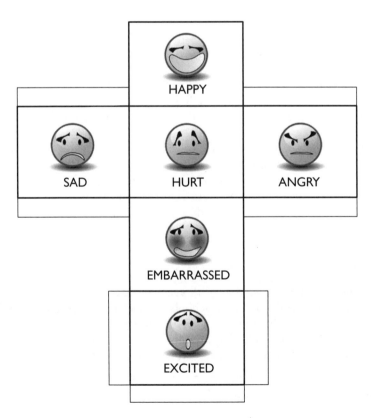

Figure 3.11 The feelings dice.

Role-play

This activity is based on an idea from McNamara and Moreton (1995) but was adapted for the purposes of the framework. The aim of role-play activities is, on the one hand, to explore if some children have experienced similar incidents at school, and, on the other hand, to make children think about how it feels to be marginalised. In this way they are likely to become more sensitive towards other children and, perhaps, change their behaviour towards their schoolmates.

Children are asked to work in groups of four. Each group is given one incident, such as those in Figure 3.12, which were developed from observations in the playground or in classrooms (Messiou, 2008a).

When developing scenarios, the real names of the children who were involved should, of course, not be mentioned. Practitioners can develop their own incidents/scenarios, based on observations in their own contexts; however, they should be very careful so that individuals cannot be identified by other students.

Incident 1

At playtime a group of children are talking in the playground. They make jokes, they tease each other and they seem to be having a good time. Close to them there is a child from the same classroom, standing, listening and looking at this group of children. The group of friends walks while they are talking, and the other child is following them but without being a member of the group. Children in the group seem to ignore that child as if it is not there.

At some point a teacher comes and asks a child from the group to go and find one of their classmates. As soon as the teacher leaves, the child whom the teacher asked to go and find the classmate turns towards that child who is outside the group and says 'Go and find . . . [name of the pupil]'. The child immediately runs to find the pupil that the teacher was looking for.

Incident 2

A group of pupils are talking in the canteen looking at a magazine. A girl who has recently arrived at school and does not speak English well knocks the table as she walks past, causing the can of Coke to spill on the magazine. One of the other kids shouts 'Hey, you did that on purpose!' She does not understand and they start making fun of her.

Figure 3.12 Incidents from a school.

Having read the accounts, students are asked to carry out a role-play based on what had occurred. Then a set of questions, such as those in Figure 3.13, is given to each group for discussion prior to a report back on conclusions reached to the whole class.

Discussions follow with the whole class and, towards the end, children are asked to consider what should happen next, using role-play.

The idea is that through this activity, and especially through the discussions that students have, examples of marginalisation can emerge in a natural way. Students may, for example, say that they have had similar experiences and this may alert the teachers to students' experiences that they may have not thought of before. In some English schools, when students carried out these types of role-play activities, teaching assistants kept notes that were used afterwards in the next step. If this is not possible, teachers can write up notes on observations after the sessions have finished, but these will be brief.

It should be pointed out that students themselves can also develop such scenarios. For example, in some schools I worked with we asked students to develop stories based on their experiences in schools. We then helped with the editing of the accounts in such a way as to make them short and easy to be read by other students. What was important in these cases was that we ended up with authentic scenarios based on students' experiences.

Here again, issues of anonymity should be dealt with carefully. Sometimes, the scenarios that students come up with involve particular individuals that could be easily identified by almost anyone from a given classroom. For example, this was the case for one incident that students wrote, which involved a boy defined as being on the autistic spectrum, describing the ritualistic behaviours that he was exhibiting as well as how others in the class were responding to these. Using such an incident in the particular class, even anonymously, would not be ethically right since everyone would know whom they were referring to. On the other hand, making students think about their own behaviours and the implications that they have for individual students is very important, and therefore these types of incident should be used in role-play situations. How we addressed this in the particular context was to use another example which was addressing similar issues – students making fun of classmates because of

---

Questions

- How does the child involved in the above incident feel?
- What else could this child do during the particular incident?
- How could the others in the group have behaved?

Figure 3.13 Questions given in groups for discussing incidents.

viewing their behaviour as being odd – but without focusing on the individual student and his ritualistic behaviours.

In general, the way in which I have addressed such challenges in schools that I have worked with was to avoid using scenarios that were written by students from a certain classroom, or even year group, with the same students. Of course, some could argue that the scenarios were year group specific but we have found that we could use scenarios from various year groups with various classes, as long as the year groups were not too distant from one another. For example, there were scenarios that were more appropriate for use with the younger year groups, compared with a scenario that we could use with secondary schools.

In essence, then, what I am saying here is that involving students in this process of writing the scenarios is very useful in terms of ending up with authentic and context-specific scenarios. For example, Incident 2 in Figure 3.12, if used in schools with homogenous learner populations where there are no students from other countries attending, might not sound relevant. Therefore, in order to have meaningful role-play activities that are likely to have an impact on students' thinking and way of behaving, the incidents should relate to their own realities and experiences. Having said that, this does not exclude the use of such incidents that might be unlikely to occur in particular contexts. In doing so, further stimulating discussions and reflection can take place. Further useful guidance about issues related to the use of role-playing can be found in Cohen and Manion (1994).

Power maps

Drawing a power map is an activity suggested by Davies (2000) for understanding democratic processes and where decisions in schools are made. Focusing on marginalisation, and whether students feel that they are involved in decision making or not, this can be a powerful activity.

Students are asked to work in groups of four, drawing a rough map of their school and indicating where they think decisions are made. On some occasions we have provided students with ready-made maps of the school. Figure 3.14 presents one example, in which students drew their own map and they highlighted the places where decisions are made, as well as the people who are involved in these decisions.

What is of most interest are the discussions that take place while students are working on these maps. I remember in one school that students immediately said 'We should indicate all the classrooms as places where decisions are made. We are asked to make decisions all the time and therefore we should show this', whereas in another school, immediately, they highlighted on the map only the headteacher's office. Again, ideally notes should be kept while the students are working on these maps, in order to have further evidence for analysis for the following step.

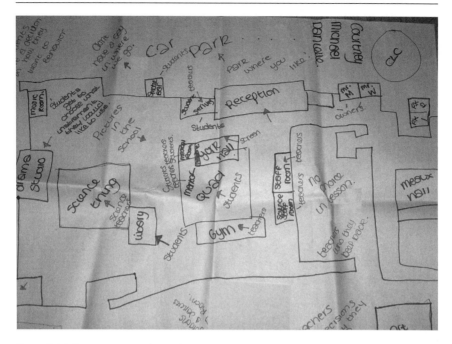

Figure 3.14 A power map drawn by students indicating where decisions are made at school and by whom.

Star charts

This was an idea developed by some students in a secondary school. They were trying to find out the extent to which the students in the school felt that they were listened to, or whether they felt they were involved in decision making. This was an idea that relates to the previous activity. So the students drew a line and the two ends were seen as two extremes (i.e. I am listened to at school versus I am not listened to at school). Then they gave star stickers to the students of each class and asked them over a period of one week to indicate what they felt by placing a star on the line. Students' indications from one class can be seen in the photograph in Figure 3.15.

In one case, it is noticeable that students placed their stars very near to the end that indicated that they felt involved in decision making in the school. Of course, the limitation of this activity is that it does not provide practitioners with the views of specific individuals. So, for example, we do not know who is the one who does not feel involved in decision making in the school. What it does provide, however, are indications of the extent to which students feel that they are not involved in decision making. This is not to say that they are truly not involved, but they feel this way. For this reason, it may be best to try this activity early on when using the framework and then, through other activities, explore these areas in more detail. It might also be used as part of interviews.

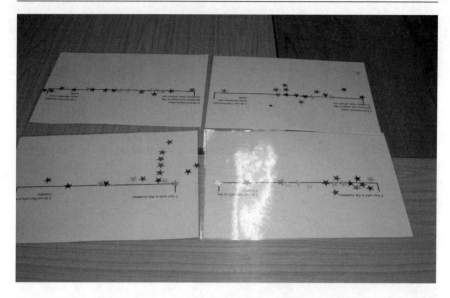

Figure 3.15 Star charts indicating how involved students felt in decision making at school.

Letter box

This useful and non-intrusive technique (referred to as the 'communication box' by the school in Chapter 2) can be used either across a whole school or in individual classrooms. Usually, the letter box is placed in a central location in the school and students are told that they can leave messages in the box in regards to what is of concern to them in the school, or things that they would like to change. The issue of anonymity has to be clarified again for this activity. One area that clearly relates to the issue of anonymity, of course, is who is going to read the messages or letters that the students drop in the box. This again can vary between schools.

In some schools, for example, the headteacher read the messages, whereas in others it was an assigned teacher. In some contexts, especially secondary schools, the school councils read the messages. I do not have any evidence that can compare the relative benefits of these three different approaches, even though in one particular primary school it was clear from what the students said that it was very important for them that the headteacher herself was reading their messages. In this case it could be argued that the students saw in the face of the headteacher the potential for change, whereas in other cases, where the school council members were reading the messages, other students might have thought that not much could be done in terms of bringing change.

The letter box can be used in a variety of ways, depending on what practitioners want to explore further. For example, we could ask students to post messages related to what they really like in schools or what they would want to do more in school – in other words, highlighting the positives that happen in schools in order to provide more of these activities. However, usually, practitioners tend to know what students like, and similarly students tend to let their teachers know what they like. Also, talking about what is positive is something that students are more likely to do without reservations. Is that the case, though, when it is something that is of concern to them? More importantly, if what is of concern is something that relates to particular adults in the school, or to individual students, or to common practices (for example, seating arrangements, or the practice of grouping students according to ability), how likely is it that students will feel comfortable in expressing dissatisfaction about these issues? This may be a particular factor with those students who are not so confident. Often these are the ones who may experience marginalisation in schools and, as a result, not be in a position to articulate their views.

What the letter box does is to act as a medium through which such students can express views in a rather unthreatening way. For example, some may hide behind a box and post their messages anonymously. With the use of technology, students can also type up their letters and then post them in the box anonymously or not, as they wish. The point that I want to stress here is that, given the focus of this book on marginalisation and its sensitive nature, this approach provides an indirect way of bringing concerns to the surface.

Questionnaires

Students' voices have often been associated with the use of questionnaires, not least because these are seen to be a relatively simple way of gathering views from a larger sample (e.g. Bryman, 2008; Cohen and Manion, 1994; Nikolaraizi and Reybekiel, 2001). Indeed, when teachers in English schools explain that they engage with students' views, they usually show a questionnaire that the students are asked to complete. Often this turns out to be the only way that these schools engage with students' voices.

There are many ready-made questionnaires that can be used by schools, each of which has its own agenda. Of course, many schools develop their own survey instruments, usually based on adaptations they make of existing ones. In some schools that I worked with the students themselves developed questionnaires themselves with a focus on marginalisation (see Figures 3.16 and 3.17).

As can be seen, the students developed different kinds of questionnaires, based on where they wanted to focus their investigations. I stress that these examples are offered not as ideal questionnaires but rather to demonstrate different possibilities.

There is extensive discussion in the literature about the strengths and drawbacks of using questionnaires in research, as well as practical advice on designing and administering such instruments (e.g. Bryman, 2008; Cohen and Manion, 1994; Robson, 1993). These sources can be particularly helpful in determining appropriate formats for getting student responses to what they

Marginalisation - Feeling left out

As part of our research project, we are looking into marginalisation in schools. Answer the questions below honestly and fairly to help us get an overview of how pupils feel in lessons, around corridors and on playgrounds at our school.

	Circle <u>only one</u> each time ☺ ☺ ☹ I agree I don't know I disagree			Additional comments
I see people being left out in my classroom	☺	☺	☹	
I choose to work on my own	☺	☺	☹	
When I am in lessons everyone is joining in	☺	☺	☹	
When I am in school I feel safe and that I belong	☺	☺	☹	
On our school playground I don't see people being left out	☺	☺	☹	
Marginalisation doesn't happen at our school	☺	☺	☹	
I feel included at my school	☺	☺	☹	

3 Stars:
Write three positive things about our school:

√
√
√

Wish:
Write one thing you think our school could improve to make more people feel included:

Figure 3.16 A questionnaire developed by students in a secondary school.

are experiencing in schools, and guidance on how they should be administered efficiently. However, whereas constructing appropriate questions or statements when developing a questionnaire is relatively straightforward, analysing the returns can be more challenging, as discussed in the next chapter.

Questionnaire

Read the questions below and tick the box with your answer (do not write your name on the sheet!)

	Yes	No	Don't know	Sometimes
Do you have friends in your class?				
Do you sit with your friends in your class?				
Do you get on well with everybody in your class?				
Is there anybody who doesn't sit with a friend?				
If there is a new student in the class do you invite them to sit with you?				
Do you get on well with your teachers?				
Do you have to sit in a seating plan?				
If someone is sat on their own would you let them sit with you?				
When/if you sit on your own do you feel upset?				
When/if you sit on your own do you feel left out?				
Do you go with your friends if you have to work in a group?				
If you had to work with other people that you don't usually talk to, would you feel awkward?				
In the school, where do you feel most safe?				
In the school, where do you not feel as safe?				

Figure 3.17 A questionnaire developed by students in another secondary school.

Of all the disadvantages that are mentioned, perhaps the one that does not really apply when using questionnaires with students as part of the framework is the danger of low completion rates. Usually, when questionnaires are given in classroom contexts by practitioners, or by student co-researchers, it is likely that most pupils will complete them. Of course, you may get some students who might not want to respond and others who will not fill in the form carefully, but the likelihood of getting completed questionnaires back is relatively high, based on my experience.

Including everybody

The methods and techniques that I have described can be used with all students. However, it has to be acknowledged that many of the activities rely on writing or speaking skills, and therefore might prove to be a challenge for some students, such as those who experience communication difficulties, or those defined as having severe learning difficulties or being on the autistic spectrum.

However, my experience is that these methods and techniques can usually be modified in order to be made accessible to all students. Usually this is done through the use of visual cues. More ideas about this can be found in various sources (for example Lawson, 2010; Lewis, 2002). Furthermore, activities such as the use of visual images have been found particularly successful with students who have difficulties expressing their views verbally. In addition, as mentioned earlier, observations can be used with all students too. Finally, some activities can be completed with the support of additional staff who work closely with individual students. It has to be made very clear to such support staff, though, that it is the voice of the individual pupil that we are interested in, not what the support staff thinks that the student wants to express.

Combining methods

As I have stressed, all the methods and techniques that have been described in this chapter can be used by practitioners, or even by students themselves where they take the role of co-researchers. With appropriate adaptations, they can also be used for purposes other than exploring issues related to marginalisation. So, for example, they could be used to explore students' views about curriculum issues, such as reading or maths, or about the way that the playground is organised.

Usually it is helpful to combine methods, rather than relying on a single source of information, since this might be limited. For example, Dockrell and colleagues (2000) argue that the use of drawings on their own for making inferences about a child's personality or emotional state is likely to be unreliable, since, for example, a child may draw a person crying for many reasons. This reinforces the importance of using multiple ways to try to understand the way children feel and think about their experiences in school.

The use of multiple methods in social science research is referred to as triangulation. This is viewed as a way of ensuring validity in respect to data that is collected (Creswell and Miller, 2000; Lincoln and Guba, 1985; Maxwell, 1992). Taken from the field of map making, the term 'triangulation' means that something is examined from a variety of angles in order to form an accurate picture of the terrain. In relation to my focus in this book, however, the important point is that by offering different possibilities for children and young people to express their views we are more likely to gain authentic evidence of what is in their minds.

Summary and conclusions

As we have seen, there is an extensive range of approaches that can be used in order to 'open doors' for students to express their views. Some of these can be used with groups of students, whereas others are more appropriate for use with individuals. It is up to those who adopt the framework to decide which approaches to use, but, as I have pointed out, it is good to combine methods to have stronger evidence in our hands.

Though the use of the above methods and techniques through the first step of the framework is very important, what is of most importance is what happens with the information gained in this step. The next chapter deals with this issue of looking closely at the data and information gathered.

Chapter 4

Looking closely

Bringing concerns to the surface

This chapter discusses the importance of stopping to think about the reactions of pupils to the experiences they have in school. In essence, Step 2 of the framework involves looking closely at data gathered during the first step in order to generate information that can be used to stimulate further discussion. Ideas of how to make sense of the data gathered, as well as how to analyse and interpret them, are discussed. In addition, consideration is given to how this analysis can be used as part of ongoing school development processes, to benefit both students and practitioners who work in very busy contexts. The importance of involving colleagues and others as critical friends in this process is also discussed.

During this step, teachers or students co-researchers have to single out extracts of data and information to be further analysed in step three of the framework. In addition, where appropriate, individuals who might experience marginalisation are also identified. Decisions on what should be singled out, and the ethical dimensions of such decisions, are discussed in detail, using specific examples to illustrate the fact that none of this is straightforward.

Approaching Step 2

As I explained in the first chapter, though the framework suggests a very specific process, within that process there are varying ways of approaching each step. This particular step has been used in a number of ways in different school contexts. For example, in one particular school, because of time constraints, each of the classroom teachers chose to look at the information gathered individually. They then presented their initial reactions to their colleagues in staff meetings. In other schools, all the year group teachers looked together at the data gathered, and, in other contexts, all the teachers involved with particular classes looked at the data together. It should be noted here, that, although there is not a single way of approaching this step, getting others involved who have not necessarily been involved in the process of data gathering can be very beneficial. The key aspect is to get those involved to think critically about what information can be extracted from the data. The involvement of more people in an engagement with the data to bring a critical perspective to what has been gathered in the previous step is likely to be very helpful, where this is possible. However, if this is not possible, sharing of some of the data and information with others will be achieved in the following step.

Before one starts to look closely, the data need to be organised. Some of techniques produce data that do not really need any sort of organising, as for example when using the message in a bottle. However, with other activities time might need to be set aside to organise the data gathered so as to be in a position to look at it closely. One such example is information from interviews. Ideally, interviews should be recorded and transcribed afterwards, or sections of the interviews can be transcribed. Whereas this is usual when the framework is used by researchers, it might not be feasible when it is used by practitioners in busy school contexts. In some schools, teachers made only brief notes after interviews with students in order to have a record of what had been expressed by them. In a school where we involved a university student as a co-researcher, transcription did take place and, therefore, we had the exact words of the students and we could identify what was of concern. In that respect, having an outsider carrying out this task was very useful.

The aim at this stage is to look closely at the data in order to, on the one hand, identify students who may be experiencing some form of marginalisation and, on the other hand, bring to the surface issues that might be the potential causes of marginalisation. Following this initial analysis, the idea is that segments of data that are of potential concern should be singled out in order to share these with more staff and students during Step 3. This selection of data should be made very carefully, in such a way as to avoid identification of any individual student by other students at any stage.

In what follows, examples from various school contexts will be used to illustrate how this process can work in practice. First of all, I provide some general principles that should be taken into account when carrying out this initial analysis of data and selecting what material to use during the next step. I then go on to offer examples of how data generated through some methods and techniques were analysed.

General principles

Systematic data analysis is a very time-consuming and thorough process, as researchers know very well. Usually teachers in schools cannot afford the time to go through this kind of detailed process. Therefore, it has to be made clear that what I am trying to offer here are some general principles for staff to use when looking at data in the first place in order to make sense of it and decide what to use during the next step. In particular, tactical decisions about which segments of data to use are an issue that both practitioners and researchers will have to deal with. This will be discussed here through the use of specific examples, once again stressing the importance of addressing the ethical dimension.

When researchers decide to use the framework, they can certainly follow a more systematic form of data analysis. This is likely to include assigning codes to the data and developing categories, for example, for data gathered through observations and interviews following the guidelines provided by Miles and Huberman (1994), Silverman (2001) and Strauss and Corbin (1990). Of course, there are well-established procedures for analysing data statistically, such as information gathered from questionnaires (e.g. Bryman, 2008; Cohen and Manion, 1994). However, this more detailed kind of analysis is not the main purpose of this book. Rather, the aim here is to enable teachers – or, indeed, student co-researchers – to think in more detail about the data gathered during the previous step, and how they can start drawing some initial understandings.

Working with schools over a number of years has led me to develop the following broad guidelines, which have proved to be useful when looking at the data collected through the first step. Specifically, the initial analysis should look to identify:

- statements and issues seen to indicate matters that are a cause for concern
- extracts that seem to be particularly interesting and could provoke discussion if used in the next step
- issues that need further exploration and
- themes that are frequently mentioned by students.

In what follows, I refer to specific examples of how this step has been approached, making reference to these general guidelines as I proceed in exploring each account. In so doing, I have chosen not to present each of the methods and techniques separately and how the data gained from these can be analysed and interpreted, since this seems unnecessary. Instead, I use examples that involve a number of methods to illustrate how this step can be approached. Throughout, I emphasise the importance of looking at the data critically – in the sense of considering different possible interpretations – and recognising the complexities that this process brings.

Thinking about the data

Focusing on matters of concern

Most of the methods and techniques described in Chapter 3 produce qualitative data. Usually such data come in the form of written statements, interview extracts or observation notes. In what follows, I use examples to illustrate the issues involved.

I will start with an example that involved the use of the message in a bottle activity. When practitioners are looking at the material from this activity, they have to focus on those messages that are perceived to be of concern, such as those in Figure 4.1.

- I would like my classmates not to make me cry all the time.
- I would like my teacher to stop telling me off.
- I would like to change school.
- I would like everybody to stop beating me.
- I would like to have friends to play with at break time.
- I would like the teachers to be fair with all the children.

Figure 4.1 Messages that can be considered to be of concern.

The students who expressed these views are possibly experiencing marginalisation of some kind, even though, as I have argued previously, they should not be taken at face value. Rather they should be seen as indicators of possibilities that at least need further consideration. In essence, the messages give insights into students' feelings and thinking at particular moments, as well as pointing to issues that might be making some students feel marginalised within a school. Here is where the anonymity issue becomes a problem for those who are looking at the data. If students have chosen not to write their names, then it means that we cannot know who has expressed these concerns. However, what is of importance is that practitioners, or whoever has collected the information, should then explore this further in order to address such issues.

Of course, it should be noted that, many times, most of the messages from this activity will not be of any concern at all, for example when many students say, 'I would like to have a swimming pool in my school'. Such messages are not uncommon, as I have found in various school contexts. Whereas such suggestions are not of concern, what is important is that they do give an insight into children's way of thinking about their school. They can also be used as a way of having discussions with students of what it is possible to change.

Where practitioners choose some of these messages to share in the following step of the framework – when a deeper level of analysis takes place – they should be careful to avoid identification of the writers. So, for example, in one school that I worked with, a student wrote: 'I don't want to be taught African dances, because I am not good at it and the others make fun of me.' When the teacher and I were looking at the messages, I thought that it would be a good idea to use this message in order to make students think about their behaviour and the impact that it had on the particular student. However, the teacher disagreed with me, since she said that the students would definitely identify who expressed this concern, since the message was so specific, and that, anyway, there was only one student who did not like African dances in the class. Of course, though the student did not disclose his name, the teacher immediately knew who said it. Therefore, the teacher thought that using it with all students in the next step would draw attention to the particular student in a way that would possibly bring more negative remarks from some of his classmates. As a result, the teacher chose not to use this message in the next step. However, for her, it was important to see the effect that the specific practice used in the school had on the student. She was aware of the fact that the student did not like African dances but she was surprised that he wrote this as the only thing he would like to change in school. Therefore, this closer look at the data made her understand better how this student felt and, consequently, pushed her to think further in terms of what he could do in order to address his feelings.

Two general issues arise from this example. First of all, as we have seen, students can be descriptive in their messages in ways that disclose their identity. This can be challenging if this information is chosen to be used with others in the following step. One way to address this issue is to use the framework across a whole school rather than in one class, a strategy which has many advantages. In this way, mixing messages from various classes to be shared with different groups of students becomes possible. The fact that these come from different classes should be made clear to the students from the beginning of the third step, in order to prevent them from trying to identify who wrote each message.

The second general issue that arises is that of the importance of collaboration when looking closely at the data. In the specific example, the insider's knowledge – that of the class teacher – was vital in deciding not to use the student's message with other students. Equally, what was very important was the fruitful conversations that took place when we were looking at this information together. We both thought that the message was very interesting. The teacher, in trying to explain why the student felt like that, insisted that the reason he did not like any sort of physical activity was because he was overweight, and therefore there was not much the school could do to change it. However, I drew the teacher's attention to the fact that he did mention the others making fun of him. Therefore, the reason that he did not like African dances could be not because he was overweight but, as he had explained, because others were making fun of him. These discussions led us to look closer at information from the other sources that we used in the class, with a particular focus on the individual student.

Interestingly enough, in this same class we used sociometric measures and this student was found to be the most popular to work with, possibly because he was seen as a successful student. Interestingly, however, he was not very popular in the nominations of whom to play with. All of this led us to have further discussions about how we could improve the experiences for this particular boy. In this way the process led us naturally on into Step 3 and, indeed, Step 4 of the framework, where making sense of the evidence is achieved, as well as defining actions to be taken in order to address marginalisation of the particular student. It also confronted the teacher with an issue regarding what action to take. She commented: 'So, what do you suggest? Just because this is an issue that is putting one student at unease, should we stop offering these lessons when all the other students love them?' The teacher's question points to an important dilemma about what we offer in schools as we try to take account of student differences. As I explained to the teacher at the time, my personal view was that the African lesson dances should not stop. There may be lots of things that we do in schools that some students might not like, or that might make them feel uncomfortable. At the same time, such experiences may be important for them educationally. Are we supposed to stop offering such lessons because of the opinions and reactions of individuals within a class? My argument is that what we should be doing first is to find out what makes it difficult for those individuals, as we did with this particular student by listening to what was making it difficult for him, and then to look at finding ways to make possible changes where needed, at multiple levels, in order to address such issues.

This dilemma relates to the 'organisational paradigm', discussed in Chapter 1, in the sense that it throws light on the significant challenges facing schools that attempt to restructure their provision in response to student diversity. At the same time, it relates to the 'interactive' position, which argues that educational difficulties arise out of interactions between the characteristics and preferences of individuals and the way a learning context is organised (Frederickson and Cline, 2009).

Even though these examples that involved the 'message in a bottle' idea were ones that brought to the surface issues of concern, on other occasions frequency, along with issues that might be of concern, can be used. In another school it was noticeable how many students mentioned that the way the playground was divided among the different year groups was unfair. For example, many of the younger students wanted to have the pitch in order to play football at least once a week. However, it was available solely for older groups of students every day. Therefore, though this issue was singled out because it was occurring frequently, it could not in itself provide concerns about the marginalisation of individuals. In other words, it does not necessarily mean that all those students who expressed this view were experiencing marginalisation, even though this could have been the case for some of them. However, I perceived these as areas of concern at a more generic level that should be further explored.

Similar to the messages in a bottle are the notes that students post through the letter box activity, even though they are lengthier most of the time. Again, the idea is to isolate extracts that are of concern. However, as with the messages in a bottle, some of the issues that emerge through this activity may not be of any concern.

As I explained in the previous chapter, whom the letters are addressed to is important. In some instances the members of the school council read the letters, whereas in other schools the headteacher or a team of staff take on that responsibility. Therefore, those involved in this step have to decide which sections of the letters they would like to single out in order to share them with others in the next step. Again, issues of anonymity have to be kept in mind at all stages.

Comments posted in the letter box can be quite challenging. We have come across letters which were quite revealing and, indeed, upsetting at the same time. In one school, for example, even though students were asked to focus only on school issues, a girl disclosed in her letter that she was being physically abused by her mother – and she identified herself too. Such information raises vital ethical dimensions, as well as having potential legal implications. What is important in such cases is that senior colleagues should be informed immediately, and each school, using whatever safeguarding regulations exist, must act accordingly. What this also highlights is that such a simple technique allowed this girl to ask for help. Up to that point she had not disclosed that information to anyone in the school.

In another school, where practitioners were looking at material gathered through observation, one teacher's notes were thought to be drawing attention to areas of concern that related to the marginalisation of individual students (see Figure 4.2). Therefore, her colleagues wanted to use it in the following step of the framework.

Incidents like this one are not uncommon in school contexts and such notes can lead to fruitful discussions amongst practitioners. In this particular case, the teachers involved explained that it enabled them to discuss how to deal with such incidents and, more generally, to address the marginalisation of particular individuals by other students during lessons. As one can imagine, there were teachers who took the view that there was not much that could be done. In fact, some argued that they could understand why some students might not want a boy like Matthew to take such roles as the one of reporting back to the whole class. Their argument was that, since some students are not very articulate, they would not represent their groups fairly, and that is why they did not want to give them such roles. Such a view, of course, created much debate among the particular group of teachers, with some rightly emphasising the fact that unless you give all students such opportunities they are not likely to develop in that respect. What is important is that looking closely at this incident led them to discuss how they could address such stereotypical views amongst students – and clearly among some teachers too – since such behaviours could be seen as marginalising individual students within the learning process.

Children are working in groups in the classroom. The teacher asks children to decide who is going to report back to the whole class what they have been working on. In one group Matthew says, 'I want to report back to the class.' Immediately Nicholas says, 'I am going to report.' Matthew says, 'But I want to report too' and Nicholas says, 'No. You are going to say nonsense like always.' Another pupil in the group agrees by saying, 'Yes, Nicholas should report back to the class. You are going to say nonsense' (talking to Matthew). Matthew says again, 'But I want to report too.'

That moment the teacher approaches their group and asks them, 'Are we OK here?' Nicholas says, 'Yes, and we have decided who is reporting back to the class. Me.' Matthew looks without saying anything.

Figure 4.2 Extract from observation notes.

This particular group of teachers decided to share the account of this incident in the next step, in order to enable students to think about their own ways of behaving and the implications that this might have on certain individuals. As I have argued, the difficulty in choosing what can be shared lies mainly with the problem of maintaining the anonymity of the individuals involved. Since we are trying to deal with marginalisation, the examples might be more unusual than the one given above, as well as being distinctive in such a way that might lead individuals being easily identified by others, as was the example of the child defined as being on the autistic spectrum that was mentioned in the previous chapter. Even in the above example, it could be argued that if it were used with the same group of learners, Matthew would probably have been identified by the rest of his class.

A similar difficulty occurred when it came to the use of an extract from an interview with a boy, Jack, which appears in Figure 4.3. When the teacher and I looked at these interview data, he immediately thought that what Jack was mentioning was important in relation to his sense of feeling marginalised. However, the teacher felt that he could not single this extract out and share it with other members of the class, since it would be very possible that the other classmates would understand who expressed the particular view. Therefore, the teacher made the decision not to share this extract with his own class, even though it provided him with an insight into the particular student's feelings. However, the extract could have been used with other students in other classes to explore how other students felt about it.

Therefore, it is essential to be sensitive enough to know what material to use and what is possibly best not to use. That is why involving others in the decision

Jack:	I'd like to go in one of the highest groups.
Kiki:	What do you mean by the highest group?
Jack:	They have low groups and high groups.
Kiki:	Which are the low groups?
Jack:	The one . . . I'm in the . . . I'm the . . . I'm in the middle group . . . the low group's what you call it . . . I don't know what erm colour it is.
Kiki:	OK.
Jack:	My group's there [shows me a certain position] and that's the highest group there and Jackson is in that. [Jackson was said to be the best student in the class.]
Kiki:	So that's the lowest one, that's there that you showed me at the front, yes . . . and you want to go in the highest, I see. And why do you want to go the highest group?
Jack:	'Cause everyone always bullies me on my table.

Figure 4.3 Extract from an interview with a student.

about what is to be shared with others for the following step can be so helpful. I would add that this is even more vital for external researchers. In this particular instance, if the researcher had been looking at the data by himself/herself, it is likely that he/she might have not known that others would be in a position to identify Jack.

Decisions regarding the information gained through some methods are far more straightforward. For example, in some schools we used questionnaires. The size of the school, and whether the questionnaires have been administered to the whole school or not, determines the complexity of the analysis. For example, if a questionnaire has been used only with one particular classroom of thirty students, then the analysis is more straightforward rather than having to analyse a questionnaire for a whole school of 800 students. In some schools members of staff took the initiative to analyse the responses from the questionnaires, whereas in others teachers analysed the questionnaires in collaboration with students. In some cases the kind of analysis that took place simply involved turning students' statements into percentages. In a secondary school, the staff analysed the questionnaires in maths lessons and looked at comparisons between statements, and, in so doing, generated graphs and bar charts to illustrate patterns in the data. In this way, the teachers were able to use the analysis of questionnaires as a useful topic within their lessons. As a result, their students engaged with meaningful data, rather than just working with random numbers. This was an excellent way of incorporating the activities of the framework into the schools' day-to-day activities. This information was then shared with others in the next step of the framework.

Emerging issues

Many of the methods and techniques described in Chapter 3 produce narrative accounts, some quite lengthy, as is the case for observation notes, for example. Others tend to generate briefer accounts, as is the case with notes kept during role-play, circle time or power map activities. Often the issues that we are looking for at this step are identified at almost the same time as the activities are taking place, since it is likely that practitioners will have kept notes about issues that were interesting for further exploration. For example, during one particular role-play activity it emerged that students felt that their teachers did not fully listen to them in school. The discussion that took place among students was summarised by the teacher who was observing, and then it was chosen to be shared with others in the next step in order to explore this issue further.

The information gained through the use of visual images is of a different nature, and may include artefacts of various types, alongside the students' narratives in captions. Again, in a similar way to the activities mentioned above, at the same time that the students are preparing and presenting the posters, some initial form of analysis is taking place as the observer notes down the views of the students. In such contexts, deciding what to note down is critical to the process of identifying areas of concern, or ones that deserve further exploration.

However, this process may well continue later, as those involved look closely at the photographs, deciding which ones to use. On the other hand, in many cases practitioners, or students acting as co-researchers, may use the whole poster as a way of stimulating further discussion, possibly amongst groups of students. On such occasions, I have found it is more helpful not to have any captions, to let other themes emerge just by allowing those involved to interpret the pictures and the messages that they might give. We will come back to this issue in the following chapter, when a specific example is provided showing how visual images were further analysed by sharing them with others.

Focusing on individuals

A method that allows us to focus directly on individual students is the use of sociometric measures. After the students give their nominations, practitioners have to put that information on a table in order to identify those who are likely to experience marginalisation in school. Figure 4.4 presents an example of the table showing the students' nominations of whom they would like to play with.

The idea is that teachers have to identify the members of the class who have not been chosen by any child to play with or to work with. Putting the information on the table makes this task easy. As we see in Figure 4.4, in this particular class three students did not receive any nominations (Mark, Mike and Carol). As I explained in Chapter 2, using tables instead of developing a sociogram of the data was found to be easier for practitioners. However, some schools did

Names	John	Mel	Simon	Peter	Alan	Andy	Mark	George	Alex	Andrew	Oliver	David	Mike	Joanna	Mary	Clare	Jeannine	Ann	Carol	Liz	Sue	Helen	Teresa	Cathy	Susana	Rachel	Shirley	Julie
John		*						*	*																			
Mel	*			*				*																				
Simon									*	*										*								
Peter																*	*	*										
Alan			*					*	*																			
Andy	*	*																										
Mark												*						*		*								
George																												
Alex						*		*				*																
Andrew		*						*				*																
Oliver	*		*		*																							
David		*			*							*																
Mike	*							*				*																
Joanne				*																			*			*		
Mary																		*										*
Clare																		*		*								
Jeannine		*														*		*										
Ann	*														*	*												
Carol																		*							*			*
Liz				*																								
Sue														*										*				
Helen																								*				
Teresa								*						*												*		
Cathy																									*	*	*	*
Susana																							*	*		*		
Rachel																								*	*		*	
Shirley																								*	*			
Julie									*											*								
	3	4	3	4	1	3	0	1	5	4	1	6	0	1	1	2	3	5	0	3	2	1	2	4	3	3	3	3

Figure 4.4 Table with students' nominations regarding whom they would like to play with.

produce sociograms as well and, of course, engaging with the data in a visual form can provoke interesting discussion, as those involved speculate about explanations of the social dynamics that seem to be involved.

What is interesting is that we found that, on many occasions, there were quite a few students not chosen by anyone, as well as others who were nominated by only one classmate. In addition, many times teachers were surprised with the results of the sociometric measures and found it interesting that some particular individuals had not been nominated by anyone, whereas for some other students with no nominations this was not at all a surprise to the teachers. Again, looking at the tables or visual presentations of the data with other colleagues led to useful discussions, as we saw in the example in the first chapter.

It has to be noted that sociometric measures are not without criticisms. For example, as I have discussed elsewhere (Messiou, 2002), the extent to which sociograms provide us with valid or invalid data is debatable. I am in a position to comment on this because of an incident that happened at one school where I carried out research. What happened on that occasion was that, after I had completed the interviews with all the children, a girl approached me and asked me to change her second choice of whom she would like to play with, since she was not a friend with that girl any more, and she would choose someone else instead. This suggested to me that sociometric measures can provide us with only a rough picture of children's relationships, at the particular time they are used. Of course, this argument can be made about other types of data collection, including interviews, questionnaires and observations, for example. All these methods provide us with data relevant at the time of the investigation, which might well change over time. Nevertheless, what I felt was that the time between this girl's original choice and the changing of this choice was particularly short.

It is worth adding here that, based on her work with sociometric measures, Ashley (1992) mentions that high-status children seem to make choices based on fact (i.e. their actual friends), whereas lower-status children appeared to make their choices based on wishful thinking (i.e. children they would like as friends). Therefore, she argues, results of sociometric measures should be treated with caution.

Even though there are these potential drawbacks in relation to sociometric measures, I view them as another valuable source of information that can help in the triangulation of data in order to identify children who possibly experience marginalisation, but I repeat that they should not be taken at face value in any case. At the same time, sociometric measures can point us towards a need for closer observations of particular individuals in order to explore if what sociometric measures are indicating is a reflection of the true picture. Going back to the instruction given for choosing classmates (i.e. 'Choose three whom you would like to play with or you would like to work with, if you could choose'), as well as the point made by Ashley (1992) about the differences between high-status and low-status students' choices, it could be argued that the nominations of some students might not be representing the reality but might be only their wishes (since the instruction is pushing towards that direction anyway). However, these could be explored further to identify whether they have provided us with the true picture or not. In addition, when using sociometric measures with the specific instruction, we are not just interested in what is actually happening; equally important is how students feel. In other words, when we identify individuals who have not been chosen by anyone, it is possible that these individuals are not liked by others in a given context and possibly this would lead to their marginalisation. That is why I still consider the information gained through sociograms as invaluable.

The tables that the teachers complete are to be used only by them and should not be used during the next step, in which students also take part. Sensitive information is represented and, of course, this must not be shared with students. I should add that, for the same reason, I have never used sociometric measures in schools where students were acting as co-researchers.

Some further issues to consider

As I continually stress, the realities of each school will determine how the framework will be used, as well as how this particular step will be handled. As I explained earlier, some teachers will look at the data that are collected on their own in order to decide what is of significance and what deserves further exploration. In other contexts, where the timetable allows for further flexibility, groups of colleagues will have the opportunity to sit down and look at the data together and make decisions collectively. Where students have acted as co-researchers, this exchange of thoughts will be achieved when students look at the information together. In some schools, where the students acted as co-researchers and where we had adults facilitating the process, this analysis was done in collaboration between adults and students. This is the ideal but it may not be possible in all school contexts.

It should also be noted that, in some cases, people from outside the school were involved in this process, such as researchers who were facilitating and providing support for the process. Having outsiders available during this step can bring a fresh perspective to the analysis of the data, since they are not familiar with the students, nor with the circumstances of a given context.

On another occasion I had two schools working at the same time. Whereas students and staff in each of the schools were collecting data in their own school, they were brought together at this second step of analysis. Bringing the two schools together seemed to be a powerful factor, both for students as well as for the practitioners, in helping them to look more critically at what was happening in each context. For example, through comparing the power map activity from the two schools it became evident that the students in one of the schools did not know the name of their headteacher. This was in contrast to the other school, where students knew the names of all the senior management team members and were very clear in regards to the roles that these people had. This came as a surprise to the members of staff involved, who, unsurprisingly, assumed that students would know the name of the headteacher.

Of course, where more than one school is involved, care has to be taken to avoid competitive comparisons. This is something that has to be explained at the beginning of workshops that bring students and staff from different schools together. So the opportunity should be seen as a way of learning from one another, and critically thinking about one's context, rather than as a way of making comparisons.

Summary and conclusions

This chapter has focused on the second step of the framework, in which participants look at the data gathered in order to carry out an initial analysis and identify areas of concern, or individuals who might experience marginalisation within a given context. How the data can be analysed was discussed through the use of examples. In addition, the discussion focused on issues around deciding what segments of data and information to share with participants in the following step of the framework.

Through this step, general issues related to inclusion and marginalisation may emerge, as well as concerns regarding particular individuals. However, it may not always be possible to share the actual information with students and colleagues, since marginalisation is such a sensitive issue. The challenges entailed in making these decisions, as well as the ethical dimensions involved, were discussed through the use of examples. In essence, then, by the end of this step those involved will have identified a set of information that reflects some concerns that they want to explore further in the next step.

Chapter 5

Making sense of the evidence

Sharing data with learners

Ways of sharing data and information with pupils and other staff members are explored in this chapter. The approaches described aim to show the dynamics involved in this process, and the potential that sharing such information can have on students themselves and their teachers. It is stressed that this sharing of data and information is not a straightforward process, and that it can sometimes lead to fruitful tensions in bringing to the surface issues that are difficult to discuss and deal with. This is, therefore, without doubt, a crucial step in the whole process, which, if dealt with carefully, will usually lead to the next step, that of dealing with marginalisation.

The word 'evidence' used in this step includes both raw data – interview extracts, for example – as well as information generated by analysing the data. However, in most cases, as will be seen through the examples used, extracts of raw data that were singled out in the previous step are shared with staff and students during this step.

In the title of the step, the term 'learners' is used deliberately. As I have said, at this stage extracts from the data, and information derived from it, are usually shared both with students and practitioners. Those who share the data are those who collected it. As I have explained, this could be teachers, support staff, external researchers, or students working as co-researchers. The important point is that, during this step, *all* of these stakeholders take on the role of learners: those who have collected the data have much to learn by listening to how others interpret what is happening in the school; and, at the same time, those looking at the data for the first time are also learning through this engagement. Often, such processes lead to fruitful dialogues that can often be quite challenging. What is important though, is that through such dialogues new understandings regarding what is happening in school can emerge, which, in turn, can generate now possibilities for confronting marginalisation. This being the case, the examples I use aim to illustrate how this step should be approached and how the processes involved can be a catalyst to participants' thinking.

Different approaches

As I have mentioned already in relation to the previous two steps, though they might appear to be, to some extent, prescriptive, at the same time they are meant to be used flexibly. It is, I stress, up to the individuals to determine how they approach each of them. This third step is perhaps the most flexible of all, in that there is no one way in which information should be shared with those involved.

Bearing this in mind, in what follows three approaches are discussed as possible ways of dealing with this step. Illustrative examples from schools for each of the approaches are provided. The approaches are:

1   sharing data and information within the same class
2   sharing data and information across a school and
3   sharing data and information at the individual level.

A discussion of these three approaches and the issues that arise out of them is also made towards the end of this chapter.

What should be noted here is that the aim of this step remains the same, regardless of how those involved choose to approach it: to deepen understandings around the data and information that has been gathered, as well as to enable participants to reflect on what others are thinking and feeling about their experiences in school.

Approach 1: Sharing information within the same class

The example for this approach comes from a primary school where I worked collaboratively with a teacher and other practitioners in a particular Year 5 classroom. On this occasion, I was the one who carried out interviews with the students, and everything was recorded and transcribed. I, therefore, had extracts from students' interviews that I could share with staff and students during this particular step.

Deciding on which aspects of the data to use was a challenging task in itself, as discussed in the previous chapter. The data that were going to be shared came from the same class and therefore there was the possibility that individuals could be identified in ways that created particular dilemmas. On the one hand, the anonymity of the children had to be protected and, therefore, the issues that were raised had to be chosen carefully so that others would not be in a position to guess who had expressed a particular view. On the other hand, areas of concern had to be discussed in order to explore in more detail what children thought about them, since this was the essence of this particular step.

In order to stimulate discussion, a one-hour session was planned with the whole class and the three staff members: one teacher and two teaching assistants. At the beginning of the session it was made very clear to participants, especially the children, that the aim was not to find out who said what but to discuss the issues that were brought to the surface from particular individuals. So it was agreed with the children that they would not try and think who expressed a particular view but rather discuss the issues that were brought up. Students were organised in groups of four and were given different extracts from various interviews to discuss through the guidance of a set of questions. Figure 5.1 is the set of questions that was given to each group. Afterwards the children reported back to the whole group and this led to further discussions.

In what follows I focus on some of the extracts that were used in the particular session in order to discuss some of the issues that emerged through this sharing of data. When the extracts were used, the names of the children were taken out in order to maintain the anonymity of the interviewee. Even though I had asked students to choose pseudonyms for themselves, when I isolated these segments of data to share, I considered it better not to use these.

This decision was influenced by an experience in another school where, as I came out of a room where I had been interviewing surrounded by a group of children, one of them told me, 'Kiki, I know who "Mel" is. It is Markus. I told him my pseudonym and he told me his!' And then the rest of the students started telling me other pseudonyms of students. This experience led me to decide to take out all names from extracts before using them with students. However, here the pseudonyms that the students chose for themselves are used.

The children all agreed that the boy in Figure 5.2 must feel sad regarding his work not being on display. In addition, two of the children in the particular group said that their work was never on display either. As the teacher had told me before carrying out the interviews, it was the school's policy that students' work was on display in the corridors outside the classroom.

When I was carrying out observations in the school I noticed that many children were looking at these displays during break times. Having each child's work on display can be seen as an inclusive practice that creates a sense of community, where each child feels that his/her work is valued (Sapon-Shevin, 1990). In discussion of this issue with the teacher before carrying out the interviews, she said that she did not think that students pay a lot of attention to those displays, and that most possibly they do not even know whose work is on display and whose is not. However, in the interviews I had with the students it became evident that they did take note of them and that all of them knew whose work was on display.

- How do you think the child feels?
- What could be done differently so that the child does not feel that way?
- Has anyone been in a similar situation at school? Can you give us an example?

Figure 5.1 Set of questions used to facilitate discussions in students' groups.

Kiki:	I've noticed that outside your classroom in the corridors there are some displays with people's work . . . have you ever stopped and looked at those?
Luke:	Yeah.
Kiki:	Is your work somewhere on display?
Luke:	No.
Kiki:	Was it before?
Luke:	No.
Kiki:	What do you think about that?
Luke:	Not that sure but I think it's a bit mean to everyone 'cause erm what if someone erm has done good work and they don't get to go on it . . . everyone should get a chance to go on it.

Figure 5.2 Extract from an interview with a boy.

When the above interview extract was shared during the group session, children came up with a very interesting idea in response to the question: 'What could be done differently so that the child does not feel that way?' They said that they could make a chart with everyone's names and keep a record of whose work is going on display. Then, when one child's work goes on display, they could cross out that name in order to ensure that everyone gets a chance for their work to be seen.

In the follow-up discussion we had with the whole class, when each group was presenting their ideas, one girl put up her hand and said: 'I would also like to say that it should not be just work that is nicely done that is put on display but also if you made the effort and have improved that should also be taken into account.'

The teacher immediately stepped in and said: 'But we already do that!'

One of the teaching assistants then confirmed this view (in what might have appeared to be a rather dismissive way): 'Yes, we already do that!'

The girl blushed and appeared to be a bit uncomfortable. I then said: 'This is a very good point, and your teachers say that they already do that, so that's something that you need to think about if you will be involved in the chart that you just suggested. To make sure that you do take into account if someone's work has improved or not.'

Discussing this incident after the session with the teacher and the teaching assistant, it was quite interesting listening to them defending what they do and trying to convince me that they had explained that to the children. I commented to them that I did not doubt what they said and that they had explained it to the children. I explained, however, that the evidence from the interviews, and then the follow-up discussion with children, had shown that they were either not fully aware of that or that they do not feel that this is truly implemented by staff.

The teaching assistant then commented: 'Yes, we might have to emphasise that to them again . . .'

The teacher added: 'Yes, but when we asked them to choose what would go on display, they were the ones that chose the ones that were aesthetically better than others.'

Again, it was made clear to both of them that, although this might have happened, it should be seen as an opportunity for further discussion with the children, especially when they would come up with their criteria for the chart.

The extract in Figure 5.3 is from the same class. It was taken from an interview with a girl who brought up the issue of ability grouping for particular subjects – usually referred to as 'setting' in English schools. This is a common practice whereby students are grouped on the basis of their level of attainment in particular subjects.

When this extract was read by a group of children, it became clear that many agreed with their classmate that they did not like setting. One boy in particular, who was in the lowest set for maths, explained to the rest of the people in his group how he felt unhappy with this arrangement. Interestingly enough he suggested that the teachers should at least close the doors so that the children would not know who is in which group! He then added that he felt embarrassed that he was in the lowest set.

This extract gave the whole class opportunities to express their views about setting practices during other lessons. So, for example, for literacy, children were also grouped according to attainment and again they expressed the views that they would want to work with the ones in the 'high-achieving' group. Through those discussions it was clear that students were very aware of who the high achievers were and, indeed, which of their classmates were struggling.

Through these discussions I also saw how taken-for-granted assumptions about what we offer in schools can be explored through an engagement with children's views that offer a different angle. For example, when children were

Emily:	Message in a bottle: I would like to change maths because our classes get mixed up with other classes but I would like to stay with my own class.
Kiki:	Are you staying in your class or are you going in another class in terms of the room?
Emily:	I'm in . . . I'm staying in my class.
Kiki:	How are you put into these classes for maths?
Emily:	Em . . . it depends if you're confident then you go into the higher one and if you struggle with maths you go into a lower one so they get people . . . if in . . . they don't want to mix people who are higher with lower ones 'cause they can't do the lessons em . . . it's harder for the ones who are struggling, and a bit easier for others . . .

Figure 5.3 Extract from an interview with a girl.

told as a group that setting in maths was to be used for their benefit (according to their teacher), they might have not dared to question the practice, whereas, when given the opportunity to express their individual views to an outsider in a confidential way, they offered a different view. It seemed that, under such conditions, children felt more comfortable in expressing their dissatisfaction about the matter. So, unless children's views had been heard, this issue might have gone unnoticed.

Another extract that was used on the day was that in Figure 5.4. The extract provoked extensive discussion amongst the students. In fact, other students explained that they too felt safer within the classroom, rather than going out to the playground, and that they preferred to be allowed to stay in. Some students became defensive about this view and said that there is a lot of support available in the playground for those who might be bullied, and therefore nobody should feel like this. As one boy said 'She [Vanessa] should not feel unsafe in

---

Vanessa: Message in a bottle: I would change when . . . when erm . . . do you know when we go outside . . . I'd like to stay in a bit more because when it's cold you still have to go outside . . . you're not allowed to stay in. And when we're inside like play with toys and stuff more.

Kiki: OK . . . what toys?

Vanessa: Like Monopoly and stuff.

Kiki: OK . . . do you ever do that or not?

Vanessa: When it's raining but not when it's cold but it's not very often.

Kiki: OK . . . and why would you want that, is it because it's just cold . . . is that why you want that?

Vanessa: Yeah and stay in for a bit more because outside you just . . . you . . . if you see a friend that's not your mate or something they might just come up to you and start bullying you but if you're in your classrooms they can't.

Kiki: Did this ever happen to you?

Vanessa: Yeah it was today.

Kiki: What has happened?

Vanessa: Melanie started having a fight 'cause I was playing with George.

Kiki: And what did you do?

Vanessa: Me I just pushed her . . . no not 'ard but just to get 'er off me but then she started getting gangs on me then she started chasing me.

Kiki: Did you say that to anybody?

Vanessa: I told it to one of the teachers.

Figure 5.4 Extract from an interview with a girl.

the playground. She says that she said it to a teacher. The teachers help you with this sort of stuff.'

What was important was that students, and the practitioners who were present at the session, came to realise that, no matter that there was support available in school, still some children felt unsafe and maybe there were more things that could be done in order to address these issues. The students suggested that, if there were students who felt safer staying in the classroom during playtime, they should be allowed to stay in, instead of having to go out in the playground. However, as some students commented, this would mean that they would identify themselves as feeling unsafe and, also, they would not then have opportunities for making friends and playing with other children. These dilemmas that the students discussed are illustrative of the complexities associated with dealing with different views and are also typical of the sorts of issues that members of staff have to deal with in schools. Involving students in these discussions might not necessarily lead to any immediate action; however, the level of thinking that takes place, as was the case in this example, is surely a step in the right direction. Unless voices such as Vanessa's are listened to, the issue that she was bringing up may go unnoticed.

The final example that I use here refers to one of the practices used in the particular classroom, that of the 'exclusion table'. This was a table at the front of the class where students who misbehaved were sent for some given time in order to think about and improve their behaviour. Though personally I was not in favour of this practice, I wanted to explore how students themselves perceived it. During an interview one particular boy, Jack, explained what he thought about the practice. I used an extract from this boy's interview (Figure 5.5) in order to explore what others in the class thought.

Again the extract created lots of discussions. There were students who said that the 'exclusion table' was very good because 'it teaches them [the ones who misbehave] a lesson and they learn how they should not do it again'. There was a boy, though, who said that he thought that it did not really help since, on the contrary, he felt that it makes you more angry 'sat there on your own'.

At that time the teacher interfered and said to the boy: 'Don't you remember though, when you first came to this school how you used to go there very often, whereas now you go there very rarely? Don't you think that this has helped you to understand that your behaviour was not right and would not be accepted?'

The boy did not say anything immediately and looked as though he was thinking about what his teacher had said. Then he commented: 'Yes, but I don't like it when I go there.' Discussing this incident with the teacher afterwards, she insisted that the reason why his behaviour improved was because he was sent to the exclusion table. She explained that this student had been excluded from another school and joined the class in the middle of the school year. At that time, the teacher remembered, he was quite aggressive and badly behaved.

Trying to get this teacher to consider other possible explanations why this boy's behaviour improved, such as the possibility he felt more included in the

Jack:	Oh . . . it's the exclusion table like if you're naughty then you get sent there for a bit.
Kiki:	. . . you know you've used that word 'exclusion table' . . . what does that word mean?
Jack:	Like you get like excluded from your table . . . you get sent off your table.
Kiki:	OK . . . have you ever been sent there?
Jack:	Yeah.
Kiki:	Do you like it? Do you think that's good?
Jack:	No.
Kiki:	No . . . why?
Jack:	Because like you wanna join in . . . when you're on there you wanna join in and stuff an' you're not allowed to join in you've just gotta sit there.
Kiki:	And why were you sent there, if you remember? What did you do?
Jack:	For talking really.
Kiki:	OK . . . and did you sit there for a long time?
Jack:	It depends like if you're like real bad you do but if it . . . well you can just get sent there for like five minutes or ten minutes or like a lesson or something.

Figure 5.5 Extract from an interview with a boy.

class than he had initially, or that he had some friends now than when he first arrived, was not easy. She could certainly appreciate that all these factors might have contributed; however, she remained convinced that the exclusion table was a key factor. To me, especially after hearing the fact that the boy was excluded from another school, the effects of the exclusion table seemed to be more nega-tive than positive.

In the discussion in the class session, I felt that the majority of students were in favour of this practice in a rather worrying way. This seems to relate to Quicke's (2003) point regarding students' views and the fact that researchers should not be surprised if these are conservative and reflect dominant views within a school. In a way, the students were reflecting the teacher's view. This made me think about how practices used in school can reinforce stereotypical views and promote marginalisation of individuals, rather than promote their inclusion, something that I discussed with the teacher. She maintained that the table had a positive impact on students' behaviour and she was, therefore, reluc-tant to abandon this practice. This confirms my view that, once teachers use a practice that they come to believe is effective, it is not always easy to get them to change it. However, I do believe that the particular teacher at least considered an

themselves with a number of possible methods for data collection. An exploration of the difficult concept of marginalisation was carried out, using a video clip and processes of brainstorming with the students, to relate the term to their experiences. The specific methods of data collection explored were power maps, visual images, observations and interviews. At this point ethical considerations were also discussed with the students.

At the end of the day, each of the two school groups had to come up with a plan and agree on the methods they were going to use to explore marginalisation in their own context. Flexibility was given to the students to choose any methods they preferred, or even to suggest new ways of collecting evidence. The students were also asked to choose the methods they were going to use for data collection. It was quite interesting that the students from this particular school decided to be more creative and use additional methods to the ones explored on the day. So, for example, they developed what they called a star chart (this is described in detail in Chapter 3) to explore whether students in their schools feel that they are involved in decision making, instead of using the power map activity, which they considered too time-consuming. Also, they decided to develop questionnaires as they had done on other occasions in their school.

After that first day, when the students went back to their schools, they dealt with the first step of the framework: that of collecting data and allowing marginalised voices, as well as issues that possibly relate to marginalisation, to come to the surface.

The second day of the workshop, which again took place at the university some weeks later, focused on looking closely at the data collected and planning next steps. Each school group made an informal presentation explaining how they had worked and what their initial thoughts were in relation to the data collected. Then they looked more closely at the data in their school groups, identifying emerging themes and discussing how they would share that information with other classmates (which would be the third step of the framework). During this process, even though they mainly worked in their school groups, they shared their ideas with the students from the other school, who also contributed to the refinement of their thinking. By the end of the day they also had to decide how they would share the information gathered with other students.

The group of students from the school I am referring to came up with a very interesting idea regarding the third step of the framework. Rather than going into various classrooms and sharing data with their classmates, they set up five different stations in the library, where other students could go and be informed about their project, and also explore further the views that were raised during the first phase of data collection. This idea had taken shape during the second day workshop at the university. However, the actual implementation of it was further discussed afterwards in the school and, with the help of the facilitators, the students managed to get it organised.

I observed the implementation of their strategy, and I have to admit that it was quite impressive. One student was responsible for each of the stations. Groups of six or seven students at a time were sent into the library, where they moved around the stations, taking part in different activities designed to capture their views. What has to be emphasised here is that the student co-researchers did not simply do a series of presentations. Indeed, the presentation stage at each station was rather brief. Since the aim was to refine thinking and gain deeper understandings, the students had a set of questions that they asked each group that came along. The student who was leading at each station also made brief notes in order to report back to the other members of the group for further analysis.

The five stations involved the following activities. The first station had a laptop and the students had prepared a brief PowerPoint presentation (Figure 5.6) in order to explain to the other students what the project was about and what the students had done up to that point.

At the second station, findings from a questionnaire survey were presented. Here the students presented posters with graphs and pie charts, showing in percentages what they had found out by analysing students' responses (Figure 5.7). They also asked students if they agreed with the overall findings, or if they disagreed in any way. Whilst this was going on, the student co-researchers kept additional notes.

Figure 5.6 A PowerPoint presentation introducing the students' project.

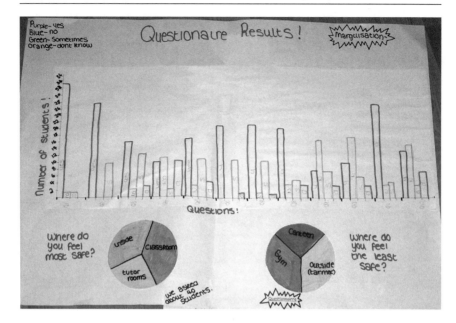

Figure 5.7 Visual presentation of the students' questionnaire results.

The students at the third station presented findings from their observations, using notes to stimulate discussion, and at the fourth station they presented findings from their interviews (Figure 5.8). As can be seen, they prepared posters where they had extracts from their observation notes and their interviews, which highlighted some of the areas that they wanted to explore further. Alongside these extracts they had a set of questions they asked each group of students to address in order to identify whether others also experienced what they observed and what they discussed in interviews with students.

At the final station, a presentation of findings from two activities was made together: from the star charts (Figure 3.15) and from the use of the photo voice technique (Figure 5.9).

The star charts were presented to the students and they were asked to elaborate on how they felt about their own experiences in their school. In presenting the visual images material the student co-researchers came up with a very interesting idea in order to see if others felt similarly to them. They prepared word cards with the different places in the school that were photographed and asked the group of students who were coming in to place them according to what they believed (Figure 5.10). It was interesting to see that some of the places that the students felt safe in school, for example, were not perceived as such by all of the other students. This might have been because these students were younger than the ones who acted as co-researchers.

In general, very interesting discussions took place during this series of activities. Some groups of students mainly agreed with what the students researchers

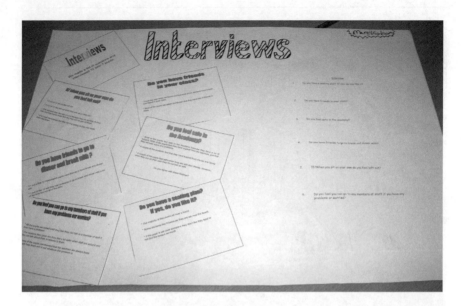

Figure 5.8 Presenting findings from the interviews.

Figure 5.9 Posters prepared by students with pictures showing where they feel safe and where they do not feel as safe in school.

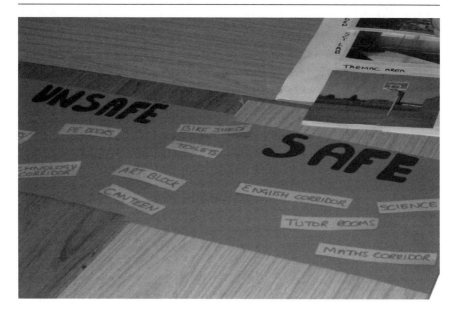

Figure 5.10 The word cards activity.

had found, whereas others challenged these ideas by adding to or refining what had been presented. So, for example, when they were looking at the observation notes – which highlighted lessons that encourage the participation of students though the use of active teaching methods – one boy said that he disagreed. In fact, he said that he felt that, although this was indeed happening in some lessons, there were others that did not require them to participate actively. This enabled the student co-researchers to add additional views to those that they had collected. Furthermore, it enabled them to see that there are multiple perspectives that need to be taken into account in trying to understand how what is on offer in the school is experienced by other students.

At the end of this step, the student co-researchers identified a set of actions that they wanted to implement, based on the information they had collected, as well as the additional issues that emerged through their consultation process. These actions are discussed in the following chapter.

Approach 3: Sharing information with individuals

As we have seen, at the heart of the third step lies the idea of opening up discussion among those involved and, in so doing, reaching a better understanding of issues that are brought up. However, given the sensitive nature of some of these issues and the ethical dimensions associated with them, as I discussed earlier, sometimes it is not possible to share such information with others. Alternatively, it may be necessary to share the information with individuals rather than with groups.

One such example was the message that a girl posted in the letter box. In her letter she explained how certain individuals bullied her outside school and went on to give specific details about classmates and how they treated her. In this particular school the headteacher was reading the letters. When he read this girl's letter he thought that he needed to act immediately and considered it important to talk to the girl individually.

He did talk to the girl and she confirmed that what she wrote was happening and gave more examples of various incidents, all outside school. Since the girl referred to specific students from her class, the headteacher considered it essential to talk to these students. When he met them, they each denied what the girl was saying. It was not possible to find out whether the girl was telling the truth or not; however, it was very important that he let them know that someone in authority in the school was aware of this girl's concerns and that, if this was happening, it should stop.

It could be argued, of course, that this could have made things worse, leaving the other students wanting to 'punish' the girl for disclosing what was happening. However, the headteacher asked the girl to speak to her parents too and keep him informed as well. In addition, he advised her on a number of ways that she could use to avoid being bullied.

The second example, although it does not directly relate to marginalisation, addresses some of the complexities associated with sharing information at the individual level. In the primary school in question, the headteacher and the teachers gathered the data. However, the headteacher led the whole process and she carried out many of the activities herself with different classes. In addition, the letter box activity was carried out across the whole school and the headteacher was the one who read all the letters from the students. She had asked children to post their letters either anonymously or, if they wanted, indicating their class and their names. Some children chose to remain anonymous, whereas others wrote their names and classes.

The headteacher told me the story of what happened. She explained that when she read the letters she found out that there was a significant number of children from a particular class who expressed dissatisfaction with the amount of homework that their teacher was giving them every day. The headteacher was surprised, since it was the school's policy not to give a lot of homework to the students, especially to the young children. These children were in a Year 3 class. The headteacher thought that since this was an issue that emerged only for a particular class, it would be quite sensitive to bring it up in a staff meeting in a way that would identify the particular member of staff. She therefore thought that it would be best to discuss this privately with the teacher.

When she started the conversation about her giving the children a lot of homework, the teacher insisted that this was not the case. The headteacher told her that it seemed that this was the way that it was perceived by many of her students, since they expressed such concerns in the letter box. The teacher looked surprised and immediately asked if this was something that only students from her class expressed. The response was affirmative. The teacher then started saying that possibly the children who wrote this were the ones who were very slow and it took them longer to complete their homework, and that was why they perceived it as a lot, and not because in reality she asked them to do a lot. The headteacher tried to tell her that, if the children feel that way, we should try and find out why, and then see what we can do about it. Then the teacher asked who had raised the issue and the headteacher told her that some of the students did not identify themselves, but indicated their class. The teacher kept insisting on finding out who the children involved were. The headteacher (who had said to the students in advance that what they were going to say would be shared with their teachers; therefore, it was up to them whether they were going to identify themselves or not) then gave her the name of a boy – who in fact, was perceived as being an excellent student and who identified himself in the letter. The teacher immediately said: 'Steve is talking nonsense! He is the best student in the class and it takes him five minutes to do his work. He is talking nonsense!'

The headteacher then became defensive as well and told her 'You know that this student would not make up things. There must be something there. If this student feels this way, there must be something there.' She also kept reminding her that there were others who expressed the same concern. The teacher kept resisting this idea, saying that she did not know where it came from.

Following this conversation, the headteacher decided to explore this further by talking to the individual student. So she said to the boy that she had read his letter and wanted to find out more. She asked him how many lessons his teacher asked them to do for their homework and how long it took him to complete it. In the discussion that followed it emerged that what he had meant was that the science teacher was giving them lots of homework, not the class teacher, and he gave the headteacher details to justify why he thought it was a lot.

After this discussion the headteacher again talked to the class teacher, who was relieved to hear that the boy meant not her but another teacher. In a way she felt that she was right and that the boy was wrong. However, as the headteacher pointed out to her, the boy was not wrong; he had something in mind but he did not express it correctly on paper and that is why it was necessary to explore the issue further to find out what he really meant. Furthermore, there were others who expressed the same view from the particular class, but did not identify themselves, so the teachers could not be certain what they were referring to.

Reflections

The three approaches highlight similar issues. In the first approach, data were shared with the same classroom members; in the second, data and information were shared among students from various classrooms; and the third approach shared the information at the individual level. What was interesting and common to all three approaches was the surprises that emerged through this sharing of data and information, as well as the changing of perceptions that took place through this process. For instance, we saw examples of how both practitioners and students, confronted with sets of views from students in their schools, revisited their own views in some cases, or in others tried to defend their own actions and ways of thinking.

In addition, some of the examples have highlighted how this step can lead to tensions. Some of these are, of course, not unusual, especially when outsiders, like me, enter into the world of schools and, in so doing, 'disturb' what is happening. We saw, for example, how on some occasions teachers felt a need to defend their actions, or even deny what children believed to be the truth. Equivalent reactions have been discussed by other researchers in similar kind of studies (e.g. Ainscow and Kaplan, 2005).

As we have seen, on some occasions such tensions can turn out to be fruitful if they enable teachers and students to step back for a minute and reflect on what is being suggested through the data. Therefore, this step should not be merely seen as a way of confirming what has been collected previously, but also as a way of digging deeper and understanding complex issues that might otherwise go unnoticed.

This third step can also be seen as a way of addressing inequalities between adults and children or young people. The framework presupposes an active participation on the part of students, and a genuine collaboration with adults. This resonates with the view of the child as a research participant, rather than as an object, with the potential to reveal many novel aspects of the contexts under investigation (Hogan, 2005; Prout, 2002).

It can be seen, too, that this particular step confronts significant ethical issues. As Morrow and Richards (1996) suggest, the biggest ethical challenge for researchers who involve children in their research are disparities in power and status. Similarly, the issue of disparities in power exists in schools too, to an even greater extent, not least because of the different roles that practitioners and students have. Morrow and Richards go on to argue that using participatory methods and encouraging children to interpret their own data are ways of minimising the ethical problems of imbalanced relationships. As we have seen, these approaches are central features of the framework.

We have seen, too, that, in trying to make sense of the evidence in relation to marginalisation, other interesting issues can emerge that point to various directions for improvements in schools. For example, the issue of the teacher assigning a heavy homework to students might not be an issue that relates to marginalisation of individuals as such; however, it can be argued that it could lead to some students' disengagement from learning, particularly the ones who might be struggling with it. That is why such issues should be shared in this step. In such ways, practitioners should be at all time alert in addressing issues that might lead to the marginalisation of particular individuals, as well as having more negative effects on all students. In regards to the specific example, that is not to say that homework should not be given, but it is about exploring the difficulties that it might create for certain individuals and searching for ways in which such difficulties can be addressed.

Summary and conclusion

The step described in this chapter is at the heart of the process. Often it naturally leads on to the final step, that of taking action to confront marginalisation. Indeed, usually these last two steps will be overlapping. The examples used in this chapter highlight the potential that the framework has, and especially this step, in facilitating processes of dialogue within classroom and school contexts.

Lodge (2005) argues that of, four types of student involvement, dialogue is one whereby students are viewed as active participants. She further suggests that dialogue 'is more than conversation, it is the building of shared narrative' (p. 134). She goes on to say, 'Dialogue is about engagement with others through talk to arrive at a point one would not get to alone' (p. 134). This can be seen in all the examples presented in this chapter. As a result, we have seen how those involved – practitioners and students – challenged their own understandings and, in so doing, considered new possibilities through this dialogue with other stakeholders in their schools.

It is likely, too, that, through this process of dialogue and reflection, levels of trust will increase and that, ultimately, this may lead to a change in the cultures of a given context. This again leads naturally to the focus of the fourth step, which is about encouraging the sorts of inclusive thinking and practices that will ultimately lead to reductions in marginalisation.

Chapter 6

Dealing with marginalisation

Encouraging inclusive thinking and practice

The final step of the framework is explored in this chapter. In so doing, ways of addressing directly the issue of marginalisation are discussed. Through the sharing of information amongst students and staff, the seeds of changes in thinking are likely to be planted from the previous step. However, Step 4 is viewed as a separate step since substantial changes in thinking, and more importantly practice, need time to take place. It is argued, therefore, that in order to deal with marginalisation, practitioners and students, working together, have to find ways to act on the issues that have emerged from following the earlier steps in the process.

Examples from school contexts are used to illustrate how engaging with students' voices had an impact on the thinking of individuals, as well as on the practices used. My main argument is that in order to deal with marginalisation we must develop this form of collaborative, evidence-based thinking and acting within particular contexts, and that this can be achieved through the use of the four-step process.

It might be expected that, in a chapter that seeks to address issues of marginalisation, a list of practical suggestions would be provided that could be used in different schools. However, as I explained in the first chapter, marginalisation is a complex issue, tied up with interconnected issues and the interaction of individual actors within particular contexts. Consequently, the problems involved are unlikely to be solved by simply lifting and reproducing responses that proved to be effective elsewhere. Rather, such problems have to be analysed within the context and thought about in order to determine what actions to take. The implication is that the circumstances of each context are likely to be determinant factors in defining the ways in which marginalisation can be addressed. That is why what is suggested here should be viewed not as recipes to follow, but only as examples of how those in other contexts have confronted issues of marginalisation.

The argument within the chapter develops around three areas: first, the idea of taking specific actions; second, the notion of listening to all, giving everybody involved a chance to be heard; and, third, the involvement of what I call 'forgotten students' in the process of data collection and analysis. It is argued that these three can each contribute to finding ways of addressing marginalisation in school contexts.

Taking specific actions

As I discussed in the previous chapter, during the third step of the framework a set of possible actions is likely to be identified. Some of these possibilities may have emerged as the discussions took place, whereas others could have been identified later on, as those involved reflected further on what had occurred.

To take an example, in one primary school mentioned in the previous chapter, one area that emerged that seemed to make some students feel marginalised was the way students' work was displayed in the school. We heard how some students felt that their work was never put on display, even though they were keen to have it seen. The students came up with a practical suggestion in order to make sure that everybody was treated fairly: preparing a chart and making sure that a record was kept of whose work had been on display. Therefore, in this instance, a possible action was determined during the third step. However, its implementation was carried out later, as I noted during a subsequent visit to the school, when it was good to see the chart being used by students.

In a similar way, we saw how, in a secondary school referred to in Chapter 5, the students who worked as co-researchers got together as a group and identified a set of areas emerging from their analysis of the data. These included the following:

- *Safety issues.* For example, the doors in a particular corridor were highlighted by most of the students as being unsafe, as they could swing and hit pupils coming from the other side. Also, a particular area of the school was identified as having stones and broken glass, which some students were throwing at other students.
- *Seating plans.* The issue of well-behaved able students (this was the phrase used by students themselves) being required to sit with pupils who misbehave came up with regard to seating plans. The well-behaved pupils felt that this affected their learning and they wanted this issue to be discussed and addressed.
- *Individuals being bullied.* Some students expressed concerns about being bullied in the school and the fact that they had not shared this with anyone else up to that point when they talked with the student co-researchers.

Most of the issues that were identified related in one way or another to issues of safety within the school. Of course, we did have the photo voice activity that focused on safety and, therefore, we expected that some related issues would emerge. However, we were all surprised – teachers, students and researchers – at the details that were emerging in regards to safety. I also came to understand that, for the students, safety was an issue that sometimes led to feelings of being marginalised within this relatively large organisation. Of course, the important thing was that this was an issue that many students were concerned about.

Subsequently, these areas of concern were presented, with appropriate supporting evidence from the data, at a meeting with the Deputy Head of the school. He was clearly impressed with the students' analysis, and how they supported this with evidence from their classmates' views. As a consequence, he tried to find solutions for most of these concerns in consultation with the students. As the students explained, through the discussions that took place at that meeting a set of actions to be taken were determined. So, for example, the Deputy Head reassured them that he would talk to the caretakers about tidying the area where there were stones and broken glass, as well as putting signs up to deter pupils from throwing them. At the same time, they all agreed that if they saw anyone continuing doing this they would explain the dangers and try to discourage them.

Perhaps the most challenging issue they raised was the point about 'well-behaved' students having to sit with 'not well-behaved' students. They explained that this was an issue that was felt by some students as marginalising particular individuals. The teachers' point of view for implementing such a practice can, of course be understood – trying to mix students in order to foster a better learning environment in their classrooms. At the same time, it can be understood that this was perceived by some students as a practice that prevented them from learning and, in so doing, seemed to push them towards the margins.

What was important in this case was that bringing the students' concerns to the surface challenged practitioners to think again about the unintended implications of their classroom management decisions. Having heard the students' concerns, the Deputy Head told them that he would discuss with the teaching staff the effect that this might be having on 'well-behaved' pupils so that they were at least aware if they chose to use a seating plan.

Later I heard that some teachers gave students the option to choose whom they would like to sit with, whereas others insisted that what they were doing was the right thing and that using such a practice would gradually improve the behaviour of the ones who misbehaved. At the same time, a few teachers chose to change their seating plans regularly, to give opportunities to students to sit with different classmates. So, even though the end result may not have been exactly what the students who expressed dissatisfaction would have liked, it certainly provoked reflection and action amongst some of the staff. I sensed, too, that the process made these students think how those who misbehave might also feel marginalised.

This account is also interesting in the way it relates to question that Fielding (2001) raises about how decisions in schools are made. He offers a set of questions that can 'enable us to apply a simple but searching interrogatory framework to arrangements and practices which seek to both acknowledge and promote student voice' (p. 133). In particular he asks '*Who decides* the answers to these questions?' and '*How* are these decisions made?' (p. 134, emphasis in the original). In this particular case, though the students raised their concerns about the seating plans, in the end the ones who made the decision about what was going to happen were the adults themselves. This is not necessarily wrong, especially since they discussed the decision with the students. Listening to young people's voices and responding to what they say is not easily achieved and there are sometimes factors that adults have to take into account in deciding on their actions. However, as in this particular example, the fact that teachers were aware of how some students were feeling enabled them to discuss the issue with the students. During these discussions, some students suggested more traditional approaches of dealing with this issue, such as having the 'not well-behaved' students sitting on their own, or at the back of the class. This allowed the teachers to discuss with students why such an approach is not really ideal and how it could potentially marginalise individual students within a classroom context even more. In this way, even though the 'well-behaved students' viewed the practice of seating plans as marginalising them, it made them think about the alternative practices as a way of marginalising others.

This is, then, an example that underlines the complexities involved in using students' voices to address issues of marginalisation in schools. It also once again draws attention to the sorts of dilemmas that often have to be faced in deciding what actions to take. In this particular case, it can be seen that different practices can each lead to individuals experiencing marginalisation of some kind. However, what I consider important is that, through this process, students – as well as practitioners – were encouraged to think in more depth about what can cause the marginalisation of individual students and, most importantly, that addressing these issues can be a real challenge.

With regards to the bullying issue that emerged in this school – which unsurprisingly is an issue that has emerged in many other schools – it seemed that where students were involved as co-researchers, other young people felt more comfortable talking about such sensitive issues, rather than sharing these with an adult. As one of the girls explained, in an interview she carried with a boy she was surprised to find out how willing he was to tell her that he was often bullied and that he wanted her to do something about it. She found it surprising, too, that he confided something like that to a complete stranger. The girl passed on the information to a member of staff who looked into this issue.

Students who worked as co-researchers in another secondary school also experienced similar responses from their classmates. As they said, when they were in the classrooms collecting data and explaining what their purposes were, some students brought up issues of bullying. They found that fellow students kept asking them: 'So what can you do about it? Will you do anything about it?'

It seems, therefore, that in such situations other students may view the student co-researchers as people who will solve the problems. Of course, in some cases this may not be possible, since the actual actions that are needed may be dependent upon adult decisions. In addition, complex issues such as bullying need time and constant effort to be totally addressed, in many cases. Therefore, student co-researchers should be prepared to deal with such responses, as it seems that other students build up expectations and see them as the ones who will deal with the difficulties they are experiencing. Most importantly, student co-researchers, using the framework with a focus on addressing marginalisation, are likely to uncover issues of which adults may not be aware, and therefore accordingly think about actions that need to be taken.

In some cases, the use of the framework led to the introduction of fundamental changes. So, for example, as a result of going through the framework process in a primary school, one of the points that were identified was that the students did not really find learning in school interesting and as a result they were disengaged. In addition, practitioners felt that some individuals were marginalised within learning situations simply because they were not given opportunities to participate. Therefore, teachers and students had discussions about the different ways in which learning could be made more interesting and engaging for all. As a result, they introduced more games within the lessons and more use of cooperative learning. In these ways, everybody was in a better position to participate in the lessons. As a consequence, the learning of particular individuals was improved in a way that gave satisfaction both to practitioners and to students.

In another primary school, it emerged that a significant number of students did not feel safe during unstructured parts of the day, for example during playtimes and lunch breaks. A number of subtle issues came to the surface in regard to this. For example, some children mentioned the noise in the dining room and how it made them feel unsafe; others said how they felt unsafe around the toilet areas, an issue that came up in many schools that I worked with; and others expressed how they felt unsafe in the school playing field, especially if left alone there. As one girl said, she made sure that whenever she was going to the playing field someone else was with her, as she was afraid being on her own. These concerns brought up by the students led the school to take a number of actions in order to address such issues. For example, the toilets were painted in brighter colours to make children feel safer and, in addition, arrangements were made so that more adults were around the toilet areas so that children would feel safer.

In this particular primary school, through the engagement with data, a group of students was identified as experiencing marginalisation during lunch breaks. Practitioners first thought that it would be good to give those students opportunities to be engaged in other kind of activities. They designed an area where these children could take part in alternative forms of play. At the same time, they did not want them to be further marginalised by being involved in activities that were different from the rest of their classmates. Therefore, they worked with particular students who were classmates of those individuals identified in order to gradually get them involved in play activities with other students as well. In this way, they saw new friendships developing over time.

As can be seen, in all these examples, practical actions were put in place in order to confront marginalisation. It has to be pointed out here that 'confront' does not necessarily mean 'eliminate'. Consequently, the actions might have to be revised on an ongoing basis in the light of new evidence brought to the surface.

Giving everyone a voice

As I explained in Chapter 1, the idea of engaging with students' views in research has become a growing trend internationally in recent years. Most of the time, the projects described in publications based around this idea entail engagement with particular groups of learners, and many times they are limited to a small number of students (e.g. Kaplan, 2008; Lawson, 2010). This is possibly owing to various practical constraints, not least that of carrying out a project that is manageable and that does not 'disrupt', at least not to a large extent, what is going on in schools. Therefore, usually a group of students is selected and researchers or practitioners explore their views and develop an argument based on what a relatively small number of pupils is saying.

What is quite distinctive about the framework is that it allows and encourages everyone to have a voice. As we have seen, it has been used in various contexts in ways that do not set limits on who might get involved; rather, it gives the opportunity to all students in a school, a year group or a classroom to be heard equally. This, in itself, takes away the stigma of marginalisation that some students might feel.

I have argued elsewhere (Messiou, 2002, 2006a) and earlier in this book (Chapter 1) that singling out individuals from a classroom context to be interviewed for research purposes can be an excluding practice in itself, whereas with the use of the framework an engagement with a wider range of views is encouraged. The importance of this can be understood if it is viewed from the students' perspective. I remember that, when I was doing my earliest fieldwork, one of the things that the students were so happy about was the fact that I would interview every single student in the school. They found it surprising that I would even talk to the young children. Later, I found that this was an aspect that was highly valued by students of all ages, in any type of school. In addition, when practitioners have used the framework in schools, they have come across similar responses from the students. The fact that many students are given the chance to be heard – rather than singling out those individuals perceived to be the most articulate and confident, who are usually asked for their views anyway – is particularly important for students.

A related issue is raised by Silva (2001), who asks, 'Which students are representing the student voice of their school?' (p. 98). This raises important issues in relation to the danger of reproducing existing stereotypes within schools. As we know, often the individuals who are asked to represent the views of the student group are those who are more articulate. Often, too, these same students are chosen by practitioners to participate in almost every event organised in the school. Through the use of this framework, attempts are made to avoid this reproduction of existing stereotypes, by giving everyone the chance to be heard. I am not, of course, arguing that just by listening to all we are addressing marginalisation. However, giving everyone the right to be heard, and valuing what they have to say, can put individuals who up to that point have felt marginalised in an equal position to the rest of the students.

Involving 'forgotten students'

In those contexts where groups of students act as co-researchers, their selection was often seen as important in addressing marginalisation. Usually, when outside researchers involve students as co-researchers, they leave it up to the teachers to decide whom to involve – indeed, I have done this in the past myself. Teachers' immediate response is to think about the ones who are the most articulate, the most confident and usually perceived as being the most 'able', who will be in a position to carry out the tasks required. I can certainly remember examples when the teachers told me that they chose the particular students because 'it will make your work easier'.

In a number of schools that I have worked with, I encouraged practitioners intentionally to use groups of students that would not be usually chosen, ones who are easily 'forgotten', possibly marginalised too. Sometimes these students are seen as being 'in the middle', not perceived as being very able, nor of constant concern and likely to receive lots of attention and other opportunities to participate in school activities.

So, for example, in one school students were chosen to act as co-researchers because they had not previously been involved in projects. At the end of the project, when I talked to the students, one girl commented:

> I felt really important. 'Cause the same people are chosen all the time and this is really annoying. It is always the high grade students that are chosen. And we are not. We are in the middle. So, when they were coming in the class to take us out I always thought 'Yes, not you this time. It is us!' And when we came to the university that was great . . . They always talk about equal opportunities but it's not. The same kids are chosen all the time. And it is unfair.

Other students expressed similar views, reflecting suggestions made by Hill (2006) as a result of a study which explored students' feelings about the methods used by adults to obtain students' views. In particular, students in that study suggested that they did not like the fact that some have more access to opportunities than others, describing this as being 'unfair'.

In another school, the facilitator of the project initially was determined to engage a group of the most challenging students in order to give them a chance to lead on something so interesting. However, in discussions that she had with me before coming to the training that was provided at the university (see Chapter 5) she expressed some concerns. Specifically, she commented: 'But they smoke and they swear, they won't sit down and listen to what you will be saying to them.' I tried to reassure her that the fact that they were assigned such a role would be so important for them that they would not want to let her down.

In the end, she did not bring to the university the most challenging group, even though the ones she chose, as she noted, were also quite lively at times. Interestingly enough, during the first day of the workshop, when she saw how they responded, she was surprised as she thought that they would not really pay attention or behave properly. At that time, her comment was that she wished she had been more daring.

It can be seen, then, that for those students who participate as co-researchers in such projects the process in itself is one way of addressing marginalisation. As the facilitators from another secondary school that used the framework told me, they noticed how particular students changed through their involvement. In this particular school, I also noticed how one boy, who would hardly say anything the first day they came to the university for training, had completely transformed through his engagement with the project. He became very confident and talkative, and he carried out his role in an effective way. This view was also confirmed by the facilitators, towards the end of the project.

In fact, in that particular school, all the students did very well. Given the fact that they were all described as being 'middle ability', both by adults as well as by the students themselves (!), it could be argued that being chosen to act as co-researchers would be beneficial.

For me, all of this relates to the concept of 'transformability', as defined by Susan Hart and her colleagues in their book, *Learning without Limits* (Hart *et al.*, 2007). They propose a move away from deterministic views of students' general ability in order to open up possibilities for the transformation of all learners. For me this is why the choice of students is very important and why it is worth giving opportunities to groups of learners who might well be excluded from other similar opportunities. In this way, we can signal to children and young people that we are not making assumptions about their capability. In other words, like Hart and her colleagues, we are refusing to set 'limits' on what they might learn.

Summary and conclusions

As I have argued, this final step of the framework should not be seen as a set of recipes to be followed in order to address marginalisation. Instead, it offers illustrations of how a number of schools came to identify a set of actions needed, and how they implemented these in order to confront marginalisation of particular individuals, as well as issues that might lead to the marginalisation of others, within school contexts. I have also argued that, apart from the specific actions that will be taken in each school, the fact that the framework enables all students to express their views is significant in terms of giving everyone involved an equal status. Furthermore, in those cases where students work as co-researchers, the selection of those students can also be significant in terms of enabling some to come out of marginalised roles in schools and take more proactive roles. The consequences for those individuals are likely to be very beneficial, as was seen through the examples I have provided.

One could argue that this final step is the most important, since this is where issues are addressed. As Roberts (2000) argues, listening to students and acting on what they raise are two different actions. My experience working with schools is that, although many have lots of evidence to present that shows ways in which they listened to their students, most fail to present what they have done after they listened to those views. Many times, they simply conclude that their students are happy, based on the evidence gathered, and they overlook issues that might be of concern to the very few. This is what this framework manages to achieve if applied carefully.

The power of the whole framework is that it enables all who get involved to be more reflective about what is on offer in school, as well as how others experience certain aspects of school life. For this step in particular, the challenge is to find ways to address the issues that are brought up. For example, how can we make students who have persistent views about one particular student, and do not want to play with them or work with them, change their perceptions and become more inclusive? More importantly, how do we make sure that this change in view persists? These questions are explored in more detail in the chapter that follows.

Chapter 7

Engaging with students' voices

An approach to inclusive education

Schools all over the world are dealing with increasingly diverse populations of students (Booth and Ainscow, 1998; UNESCO, 2010). This is, in part, because of the increased movement of populations within and between countries, and legislation that promotes the inclusion of students who were traditionally excluded from education, such as those defined as having special educational needs. As a consequence, one of the key challenges facing schools is that of reducing marginalisation amongst pupils within educational contexts. This book demonstrates ways in which engaging collaboratively with the views of students can provide a means of confronting marginalisation. As I have shown, this process can be facilitated through the use of the four-step framework I have presented.

In this chapter, I reflect further on the experiences I have described. This leads me to argue that the whole process of the framework can itself be viewed as a way of addressing marginalisation. Based on this argument, a revised framework is presented in order to capture the complexity of the processes involved. This requires us to rethink marginalisation as a concept, alongside the ways in which it can be addressed in schools. Finally, this leads me to argue that engaging with students' voices represents a distinctive approach for promoting inclusive education.

The framework process as a way of addressing marginalisation

The framework described in this book provides practical guidance to how teachers can include all of their students in the academic and social experiences they provide, by making efforts to listen to the views of their pupils. As we have seen, this approach enables teachers to reflect about the experiences they provide for their classes, as well as the practices they use. We have also seen that this can be moved in an even more radical direction when students themselves are invited to take an active approach as co-researchers. In such ways, the framework can create mirrors through which practitioners can see reflections of themselves and the impact of their own actions on individual students, as well as on their class as a whole. At the same time, it can enable students to stop and think about what they are experiencing in school, as well as think about the experiences of their classmates, and what they can do in order to address issues that become apparent. In these ways, the framework process can provoke alternative ways of thinking and, consequently, lead to changes in thinking and practice.

In the previous chapter, for, example, we saw how both practitioners and students were stimulated to think about the implications of the seating plans arrangements and the way they were impacting on individuals within the school. This process of rethinking was likely to be beneficial in regard to changing actions. Of course, I am not arguing that just by thinking about these issues changes will take place. On the other hand, it is surely more likely that the issues will be addressed than if they were simply not discussed.

In other instances there was evidence that the use of the framework led to noticeable changes in thinking and practice. This was clearly the case in the account of the girl who interviewed her classmates and found out, to her surprise, that one of them was being bullied. Though she was not the one involved in the boy's bullying, this made her become more proactive in terms of stopping this happening. What she did was to first talk to an adult in the school, after gaining the student's consent, and then, together, the student co-researcher and the member of staff thought that they should also approach individual students in order to address the issue. The element of collaboration was, therefore, of significant importance, as in most of the accounts I have provided.

Of course, bullying is less of a hidden issue in many schools that have developed policies for keeping the issue under constant review. However, as this example illustrates, for some individuals it may still be a feature of their life in school that is simply not noticed. Through the use of the framework such hidden concerns are brought to the forefront in ways that enable students and practitioners to collaborate in finding solutions.

Examples such as these show how an engagement with the whole process of the framework led to confronting the marginalisation of individual students, as well as dealing with issues that could relate to marginalisation more generally within a school. We have also seen that the actions and the changes in thinking that took place came about as a result of going through the process of the whole framework, and did not suddenly appear as a set of actions during the final step. As I have argued, in practice, the steps overlap, especially the last three, and those using the framework must bear this in mind. As I have worked with the framework in a variety of school contexts, this realisation led me to revisit the way that the framework is presented diagrammatically. Next I present this revised version and discuss how and why it emerged.

Revisiting the framework

Writing is a thinking process or, as Richardson (1998) argues, a method of discovery and analysis through which we discover new aspects of our topic and our relationship to it. Equally, research provides a means of learning as we change our ideas in response to new evidence and, in so doing, come to see things from new perspectives. In using the framework in the schools that I worked with I usually presented it in the form seen in Chapter 1 (Figure 1.2). As I was writing this book, however, I found myself occasionally uncomfortable about the need to provide accounts in relation to the boundaries of each step. As I have mentioned many times, in practice there is overlap between the steps, especially between the last three steps. I hope that by now it is clear to the reader that, although the steps provide a helpful way of planning what to do, the process in putting it into action is far from straightforward and does not involve a set of mechanical actions that have to be followed rigidly. In order to reinforce this argument, Figure 7.1 presents what I now think better reflects the processes involved.

Through this reformulation I try to capture the overlapping nature of the steps, especially of the last three. As we see, Step 1 is considered to be a distinct step in itself, in which activities are used in order to facilitate students' voices coming to the surface. Actions in relation to the other three steps can then be seen to overlap and interconnect in a variety of ways that are illustrated through the examples I have provided.

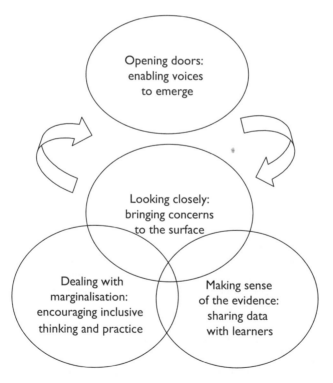

Figure 7.1 The redefined framework for promoting inclusion.

I must stress that the initial version of the framework, as presented in Figure 1.2, was the one used in all schools that I worked with. In that formulation the impression is given that all the steps are separate and discrete. Presenting that version to practitioners or students as co-researchers seemed to work effectively for the purposes of planning research projects in schools. That is why I chose to introduce it as such in the first chapter. However, I now feel that it is necessary to offer the refined version in a way that I hope will be most helpful to readers.

At this stage, too, it is relevant to explain how the process suggested through the framework relates to the idea of action research. According to Elliot (1991):

> Action research might be defined as *'the study of a social situation with a view to improving the quality of action within it'*. It aims to feed practical judgement in concrete situations, and the validity of the 'theories' or hypothesis it generates depends not so much on 'scientific' tests of truth, as on their usefulness in helping people to act more intelligently and skillfully. In action research 'theories' are not validated independently and then applied to practice. They are validated through practice.
>
> (p. 69, original emphasis)

What I am arguing here clearly relates to this definition, in that, by going through the process of the framework, practitioners and students are likely to be in a position to act in such ways as to address issues that create marginalisation in schools. Action research has also been defined as research by practitioners to solve their own problems, as well as to improve their professional practice (McKernan, 1996). This reminds us that improvement is central to action research. McNiff and Whitehead (2010) rightly argue that, in this respect, improvement does not necessarily relate to something faulty that needs improvement. Rather it should be seen as 'an ongoing process of changing for the better over time' (p. 35). In a similar way, the process suggested by the framework aims to improve practices in order to offer the best experiences to students in schools. In other words, though the emphasis is on marginalisation – and on issues that relate to it – this does not necessarily mean that there are things that are wrong in a school. On the contrary, what I am arguing is that the framework will allow subtle issues to come to the surface that might be of concern – or that can be improved – to prevent individuals from experiencing marginalisation, or, in other cases, to address issues of marginalisation that are already occurring. In this important sense, the approach can be viewed as making significant contributions to overall school improvement, albeit with a strong commitment to social justice.

There are, however, issues that have to be kept in mind in adopting this orientation. In offering a critique of educational action research, Hopkins (2008) makes the point that the specification made of processes in the various suggested action research models can be restricting for practitioners. He argues, 'the tight specification of process steps and cycles may trap teachers within a framework which they may come to depend on and which will, consequently, inhibit independent action' (p. 55). I feel that the framework I offer here, though presented as a step-by-step approach, does offer the flexibility to teachers to adapt each of the steps in a way that suits them and the reality of their school context, as the examples that I have used illustrate. I am also arguing that, through the framework, independent action is encouraged rather than prohibited.

As we have seen, actions are likely to be defined based on what emerges through an engagement with the data and the sharing of them with others. This means that the outcomes cannot be predetermined. Ballard (1999) rightly points out that research may not offer a knowledge base for 'best practice' that could apply across settings. He suggests that teaching is a complex process located within culture, place and the interactions of particular teachers and students. This being the case, I would like to stress that, similarly, the use of this framework sets out not to produce recipes to follow, but to better understand the complex processes of marginalisation and inclusion. Through the use of the framework such understandings throw light on how practices might be further developed.

I therefore view the framework as a useful tool to be adapted to fit particular circumstances, rather than as one that restricts the actions of those who choose to use it. In saying this I am also very well aware that schools are extremely busy contexts. It is encouraging, therefore, that so many teachers have said to me that they have found the framework to be helpful and feasible.

Reflecting on the design of the framework as a way of addressing marginalisation and promoting inclusion has also led me to rethink marginalisation as a concept and how it can be addressed. This is explored in what follows.

Rethinking marginalisation

As I discussed earlier, marginalisation is a complex and elusive concept. Working with schools in trying to address issues that relate to marginalisation has led me to rethink the concept, as well as issues that relate to it. In Chapter 1, I described marginalisation as being complex and difficult to define, as something that might be experienced by individuals but not perceived as such by others, as my second way of viewing marginalisation suggests. I also emphasised the fact that it can come in rather subtle forms within school contexts.

I have also argued elsewhere that I start from the belief that marginalisation is experienced by some within any given school context (Messiou, 2011), a point that is illustrated in some of the examples used in this book. Therefore, my emphasis here is not on coming up with a further theoretical definition of marginalisation, but on what should be done in schools in order to confront marginalisation, as well as prevent it from occurring. As illustrated through certain of my examples, sometimes, in order to confront issues that relate to marginalisation, relatively straightforward actions have to be taken. At other times, though, confronting marginalisation requires changes at multiple levels.

For instance, in the example about bullying, the issue was addressed at two levels: not only by working with the individual in exploring ways of how to stand up for himself and become more assertive, but also, at the same time, working with the other students as a whole group. It should be made clear here that working with the individual does not mean that a deficit view of that particular student is adopted. On the contrary, the potential of involving the individual is recognised.

One might wonder whether acting in different ways is possible to happen in all cases, given the complex nature of marginalisation. If interweaving factors – possibly including some outside the control of the school – create marginalisation, what does this imply for those within the school context? Clearly we are talking about very complex and difficult notions here. Nevertheless, it is still worth trying to address the issues that are within our reach in schools. For example, if someone is feeling marginalised because his/her family cannot afford to buy him/her stylish nice clothes and gets picked on because of his/her appearance (something that I have found happening in a number of secondary schools), there is little those in school can do to change the situation in the family. What we can do, though, once such an issue is brought to the surface, is discuss it with individuals as well as with groups of students, and ask them to reflect on the impact of their comments, or their behaviour, towards their class-mates. Role-play activities were found to be particularly helpful in this respect, in that they enable individuals to get in the position of those who receive these kinds of comments and see how it feels to be picked on about such issues.

All of this means that, in order to address marginalisation, a range of factors have to be addressed, some of which might be difficult to achieve within the walls of a school. However, there are certainly areas upon that teachers can have an impact on. For example, Banks (1993, 1998) provides a helpful map of possibilities through his analysis of five dimensions of multicultural education: content integration, knowledge construction, equity pedagogy, prejudice reduction and empowering school culture and social structure. All of these dimensions relate to the classroom and school levels. Banks explains that *content integration* refers to the extent which teachers use examples, data and information from a variety of cultures and groups in their teaching; *knowledge construction* refers to the process whereby teachers help students understand how knowledge is created with a particular focus on how it is 'influenced by the racial, ethnic and social-class positions of individuals and groups' (Banks, 1993, p. 6); *equity pedagogy* refers to the techniques and methods that teachers use in order to facilitate the academic achievement of students from diverse racial, ethnic and social-class groups; *prejudice reduction* refers to the strategies that can be used in order to help students to develop more democratic attitudes and values in order to reduce prejudices; and, finally, *empowering school culture and social culture* refers to the process of restructuring the structure and organisation of the school so that students from diverse racial, ethnic and social-class groups experience equal educational opportunities.

The ideas presented through these five dimensions can be used in order to promote inclusion in a broader sense, rather than focusing only on multicultural education. If inclusion is about enabling all learners to succeed, accepting all and empowering students in schools, these five dimensions can be used, and should be used as a means of responding to diversity. Furthermore, I see the framework described in this book as a way forward in achieving this. For example, in order to achieve content integration, practitioners could certainly rely on their own knowledge and make appropriate adaptations to the curriculum. However, an engagement with students' voices is likely to provide insightful ways forward on what needs changing. Similarly, when referring to equity pedagogy, Banks argues that teachers should change their methods so that students from diverse racial groups and both genders can achieve. What I am arguing here is that, through the use of the framework, students can make suggestions that might point teachers to possible actions that will enable them to find ways of engaging all members of their classes. Ultimately, in doing this the aim is that no student is left out.

Banks (1993) argues that 'typologies are helpful conceptual tools because they provide a way to organise and make sense of complex and disparate data and observations. However, their categories are interrelated and overlapping, not mutually exclusive' (p. 7). Similarly, the four-step process of the framework suggested in this book can be seen as a way of organising evidence and making sense of what is happening in a school. Most importantly, once such an approach is embedded in a school's work, practitioners are likely to be more sensitive about listening to what children and young people say, and sharing concerns with them in order to find solutions. I personally view the process as one that enables critical thinking about what is happening in schools, and, in so doing, facilitating changes in thinking and behaviour. As I have stressed, this is achieved through using a collaborative approach.

It would be unrealistic to present the use of the framework as a trouble-free process. The examples used in the earlier chapters highlight some of the complexities and challenges involved, as well as how those were addressed. At the same time, the examples used were based on what could be termed as 'successful' experiences of using the whole process of the framework. However, there were occasions – very few, I have to admit – when schools did not manage to get on with the whole process suggested by the framework. One such example was that of a secondary school where the facilitator, a teacher of English, was very enthusiastic and committed. At the time she had taken the role of the facilitator she had also become the special educational needs coordinator in the school. This turned out to be a difficulty, in that she had taken on considerable new responsibilities that did not really allow her to be involved to the extent that she wanted to in supporting her colleagues in using the framework. In fact, they only managed to complete steps 1 and 2.

Therefore, the issue of time should not be underestimated. Though we had a committed teacher taking on the role of facilitator, in the end, owing to a very heavy workload, she did not manage to get on with the project as she might have liked to. Clearly, enthusiasm, although essential, is not enough. What is important is that there should be flexibility to make time to be involved.

For me, in order for the framework to be used effectively within a school, a strong commitment to engage with students' voices is needed, and, therefore, leadership is a significant issue. In other words, supportive leaders, who will make sure that the process is followed and keep everyone involved committed to the whole framework, are an essential part of the success. In this context I take success to mean an authentic engagement with students' voices and the emergence of democratic dialogue amongst teachers and students, as I go on to explain in what follows.

An authentic engagement with students' voices

Mitra (2003) argues that structural issues, such as large school and class size, can increase student alienation. She also adds that separation by age and ability prevents students from learning from more experienced peers. Referring specifically to schools in the United States, she goes on to mention the pressures for proving school success as measured by test scores. She argues that all of these factors can create barriers to the kind of tolerance that is required when engaging with students' voices.

My experience suggests that similar issues apply in the English context, and I assume that they may apply in other countries. However, in some other contexts this may not be the case. For example, in a context that I am very familiar with, Cyprus, schools do not have the pressures of proving their successes through the publication of performance league tables, for example, neither are there the large school sizes found in parts of England. Therefore, the importance of context and its specifics should be taken into account when engaging with students' voices.

In addition, I would argue, that tolerance and willingness to engage with students' voices is the most determinant factor in moving forward. Based on the work that I carried out in a number of school contexts, the factor that allowed schools to truly engage with students' voices was this willingness to move forward, regardless of the surrounding pressures. Where this willingness was at a collective level, this was even more significant. In the schools that I worked with, the use of the framework often seemed to reinforce this willingness. It also allowed those involved to engage with students' voices in a way that was authentic – meaning that they truly listened to what the students were saying and acted upon the issues that emerged.

At the same time, there are other barriers that have to be addressed, some of which relate to adult attitudes. For example, Anderson and Herr (1994) argue that 'students are everywhere in schools, and yet they are too often invisible to the adults who work there' (p. 59). They also refer to the work of Fine (1991), who argues that schools engage in an active process of silencing students, through their policies and practices, in order to smooth over social and economic contradictions. Anderson and Herr continue by arguing that, 'just as students learn what behaviour is institutionally sanctioned, they also learn to recognise institutionally sanctioned discourse' (Anderson and Herr, 1994, p. 60).

These ideas relate to the subtle messages that students pick up through their experiences within a school. So, for example, Massialas (2001) refers to the hidden curriculum of a school: the learning that takes place incidentally as a result of the actions by school personnel, parents, students, as well as other community agents. In other words, students pick up messages in schools without those being explicitly articulated in any way, but they know what is expected from them in the school and what is not allowed. Therefore, it could be argued that through the way that a school operates students receive messages, and they know whether their views are allowed to be expressed or not, and whether they are valued or not.

The framework has a contribution to make here in that it aims to open up opportunities to students to express those views that they might have not dared to do so under other circumstances. However, what is of most importance is for such views to be heard and acted upon. In this respect, Fielding (2001) provides a list of insightful questions that one has to keep in mind when engaging with students' voices. These are:

- Who is allowed to speak?
- To whom?
- What are they allowed to speak about?
- What language is encouraged or allowed?
- Who decides the answers to these questions?
- Who is listening?
- How and why?
- How are those decisions made?
- How, when, where, to whom and how often are these decisions communicated?

(p. 134)

The suggested framework addresses most of these questions. As I have stressed, the fundamental idea is that all students' voices should be heard. Therefore, in relation to Fielding's first question 'Who is allowed to speak?', or even broadening this question into 'Who is given an opportunity to speak?', by using the framework everybody is given an opportunity to speak. In addition, through the methods and techniques that are used in the framework, students are free to talk about many issues that they are concerned about, albeit with a particular focus on matters that might relate to marginalisation. Moreover, the suggested approaches move beyond 'language' as such and seek to enable students to express their views in a variety of creative ways. Clearly, there are no predetermined answers to the areas that emerge; on the contrary, by listening to students we aim to develop new understandings and, as a result, be directed towards possible new solutions.

The whole framework requires a collaborative approach, especially during the last two steps. Therefore, relating to Fielding's final four questions, the idea is that everybody involved in the process is listening and decisions will be made together in order to move forward with a shared understanding. This is appropriately ethical and puts students at the centre of learning and decision-making processes.

In all these ways I see the framework as a way of enabling students – particularly those who might experience marginalisation of some kind – to gain a voice and ultimately become more visible within their schools. Through this process the empowerment of students is facilitated. As this occurs, it is likely that the school itself is transformed. As Fielding (2004) argues:

> Transformation requires a rupture of the ordinary and this demands as much of teachers as it does of students. Indeed, it requires a transformation of what it means to be a student; what it means to be a teacher. In effect, it requires the intermingling and interdependence of both.
>
> (p. 296)

As we have seen, the use of the framework employs collaborative structures, in which practitioners and students share information and, through engaging in dialogues, arrive at collective solutions for confronting marginalisation. In these ways, a greater interdependence between students is reinforced, as well as interdependence amongst students and adults. Where this occurs we see progress towards what others have defined as an inclusive culture (Dyson et al., 2004).

An approach to inclusive education

This discussion of school transformation, with its emphasis on interdependence, takes us back to the agenda of inclusive education that I introduced in Chapter 1. There I explained that the rationale for my work is informed by the 'organisational paradigm' for promoting inclusion in schools. My specific contribution is to present the case for listening to children as a key strategy for putting such an approach into practice.

The importance of listening to learners in educational contexts has, of course, been argued by many authors (e.g. Ainscow et al., 1999; Allan, 1999; Allan, 2010; Carrington et al., 2010; Fielding, 2001; Mahbub, 2008; Rudduck and Flutter, 2000). However, my argument takes these ideas a little further in that I am suggesting that listening to children in relation to inclusion is, in itself, a manifestation of being inclusive. More specifically, I suggest that, if we accept the argument that inclusion is about identifying and addressing barriers to learning and participation, an engagement with students' voices becomes essential. At the end of the day, those who experience either inclusive or exclusive practices are the students themselves. They are, therefore, in a better position than anyone else to explain what it feels like to be a learner in a given context. It follows that engaging with students' voices in an authentic way can be viewed as a potentially powerful approach to inclusive education.

The emphasis of the framework process is on how students themselves perceive what is happening in educational contexts, as well as how they feel about specific aspects of school life. More importantly, through the collaborative approach required by the framework, solutions to issues that are of importance to students can be found and, therefore, can provide schools with ideas on how to become more inclusive.

Tangen (2009) argues that engaging with students' views 'can make a powerful contribution to developing a better understanding of how equality, inclusion and quality of school life can be achieved' (p. 829). As we have seen, through collaborating with students, some complex and hidden areas might otherwise go unnoticed. In this crucial sense, an emphasis on true engagement with students' voices can be viewed as a distinctive approach to inclusive education.

Summary and conclusion

As discussed in this chapter, the whole process of the framework presented in this book can be seen as a way of addressing marginalisation. Particular attention should be given to the fact that the framework process should be seen as a cyclical process that has to become a continuing and never-ending aspect of the work and culture of a school. In this respect, schools that are using the framework will not by the end of the fourth step manage to eliminate all issues to do with marginalisation. It is very possible that at the end of the final step other issues might emerge that need to be further explored. Nevertheless, once such an approach is embedded in a school's work, teachers are likely to be more sensitive about listening to what children and young people say and sharing concerns with them in order to find solutions.

Going through such processes schools can engage in authentic dialogues with students and, consequently, create environments that are all the more inclusive. This process of engaging with students' voices in an authentic way can be seen as a distinctive approach to inclusive education.

Conclusion

Collaborative journeys

It is July 2011 and I still take the bus to work. Schools have now finished, however, and the bus feels very quiet. In many senses it makes the journey much easier and quicker . . . in other ways, it makes the journey less interesting. I wonder what all those students are doing now they are off from school. No doubt, most of them will be back in September, ready for new challenges in schools, alongside their friends and their teachers.

I sometimes still meet on the bus those same individual students that I mentioned in the introduction to this book. Over the last three years new faces have appeared on the bus, as one would expect. Students come and go in schools, in similar ways to how they get on and off on a bus. As a result, practitioners will always have to deal with different issues of marginalisation within schools, as new students arrive.

The framework is a proposal for addressing some of those issues. Primarily it is a suggestion of how students and practitioners can come closer and work in more collaborative ways. Through the framework, it is not just practitioners who are opening doors for students. Doors for discussion are opened for practitioners too.

In the introductory chapter, the recurring question that I presented was 'what more can be done in schools?' Through the examples provided in this book it is clear that there is no single answer to this question. The idea is that, by collaborating with students, possible pathways of what more can be done will be brought into sight. In this way, an engagement with students' voices can take practitioners closer to unknown areas, and even those that are perceived as known may be seen in a different light. In this sense, practitioners and students embark on journeys all the time. Those collaborative journeys can be seen as ways of reaching out to all learners and creating schools that are all the more inclusive. Indeed, engaging with students' views in schools can therefore be seen as a distinctive approach to inclusive education.

In 2010 the city of Hull celebrated the work of the poet Philip Larkin, twenty-five years after his death. Larkin was also the chief librarian at the University of Hull between 1955 and 1985, the year he died. As part of the celebrations, various events were organised and on the local buses stickers were placed with extracts from some of his most famous poems.

This struck me as being an excellent idea. I do not know how many of those students that I used to meet on the bus stopped and read them. I certainly did and it was a pleasant start to the day. One extract from the poem 'Days' read:

> What are days for?
> Days are where we live.
> They come, they wake us
> Time and time over.
> They are to be happy in:
> Where can we live but days?
>
> (Larkin, 1964, p. 24)

Listening to students and opening honest conversations with them in schools may be a way forward for making their days happy. Some of our students may have only this opportunity in schools; some may not even have this opportunity. It is our duty, our responsibility to our children and young people, to give them a chance to be heard and to act upon what they say: to make their days happy and to enable them through this participative process to build healthy happy lives and bright futures.

References

Ainscow, M. (1999) *Understanding the Development of Inclusive Schools*. London: Falmer Press.

Ainscow, M. (2000) Profile. In Clough, P. and Corbett, J. (Eds) *Theories of Inclusive Education*. London: Paul Chapman.

Ainscow, M., Booth, T. and Dyson, A. (1999) Inclusion and exclusion in schools: Listening to some hidden voices. In Ballard, K. (Ed.) *Inclusive Education: International Voices on Disability and Justice*. London: Falmer Press.

Ainscow, M., Booth, T. and Dyson, A. (2006) *Improving Schools, Developing Inclusion*. London: Routledge.

Ainscow, M. and Kaplan, I. (2005) Using evidence to encourage inclusive school development: Possibilities and challenges. *Australasian Journal of Special Education*, 29 (2): 106–116.

Alexander, R. (2010) *Children, Their World, Their Education*. London: Routledge.

Allan, J. (1999) *Actively Seeking Inclusion*. London: Falmer Press.

Allan, J. (2010) Questions of inclusion in Scotland and Europe. *European Journal of Special Needs Education*, 25 (2): 199–208.

Anderson, G. L. and Herr, K. (1994) The micro politics of student voices: Moving from diversity of bodies to diversity of voices in schools. In Marshall, C. (Ed.) *The New Politics of Race and Gender*. London: RoutledgeFalmer.

Armstrong, D., Armstrong, F. and Barton, L. (2000) Introduction: What is this book about? In Armstrong, F., Armstrong, D. and Barton L. (Eds) *Inclusive Education: Policy, Contexts and Comparative Perspectives*. London: David Fulton.

Ashley, M. (1992) The validity of sociometric status. *Educational Research*, 34 (2): 149–154.

Ballard, K. (1997) Researching disability and inclusive education: Participation, construction and interpretation. *International Journal of Inclusive Education*, 1 (3): 243–256.

Ballard, K. (1999) International voices: An introduction. In Ballard, K. (Ed.) *Inclusive Education: International Voices on Disability and Justice*. London: Falmer Press.

Baloche, L. (1998) *The Cooperative Classroom. Empowering Learning*. Upper Saddle River, NJ: Prentice Hall.

Banks, J. (1993) Multicultural education: Historical development, dimensions and practice. *Review of Research in Education*, 19: 3–49.

Banks, J. (1998) Multiculturalism's five dimensions: Interview with Michelle Tucker. *NEA Today Online*. Retrieved 24 May 2011 from http://www.learner.org/workshops/socialstudies/pdf/session3/3.Multiculturalism.pdf

Barton, L. (1997) Inclusive education: Romantic, subversive or realistic? *International Journal of Inclusive Education*, 1 (3): 231–242.

Becker, H. (1973) *Outsiders: Studies in the Sociology of Deviance*. London: Collier Macmillan.

Belanger, N. (2000) Inclusion of 'pupils-who-need-extra-help': Social transactions in the accessibility of resource and mainstream classroom. *International Journal of Inclusive Education*, 4 (3): 231–252.

Blumer, H. (1969) *Symbolic Interactionism: Perspective and Method*. Englewood Cliffs, NJ: Prentice Hall.

Booth, T. and Ainscow, M. (1998) *From Them to Us*. London: Routledge.

Booth, T. and Ainscow, M. (2002) *Index for Inclusion*, 2nd edn. Bristol: CSIE.

Bryman, A. (2008) *Social Research Methods*. New York: Oxford University Press.

Burke, C. (2008) 'Play in focus': Children's visual voice in participative research. In Thomson, P. (Ed.) *Doing Visual Research with Children and Young People*. London: Routledge.

Canney, C. and Byrne, A. (2006) Evaluating circle time as a support to social skills development: Reflections on a journey in school based research. *British Journal of Special Education*, 33 (1): 19–24.

Carrington, S., Bland, D. and Brady, K. (2010) Training young people as researchers to investigate engagement and disengagement in the middle years. *International Journal of Inclusive Education*, 14 (5): 449–462.

Casey, T. (2005) *Inclusive Play*. London: Paul Chapman.

Charlton, T. (1996) Listening to pupils in classrooms and schools. In Davie, R. and Galloway, D. (Eds) *Listening to Children in Education*. London: David Fulton.

Christensen, P. and James, A. (2001) Introduction: Researching children and childhood: Cultures of communication. In Christensen, P. and James, A. (Eds) *Research with Children: Perspectives and Practices*. London: RoutledgeFalmer.

Clark, C., Dyson, A., Millward, A. and Skidmore, D. (1995) Dialectical analysis, special needs and schools as organisations. In Clark, C., Dyson, A. and Milward, A. (Eds) *Towards Inclusive Schools?* London: Fulton.

Cohen, E. G., Lotan, R. A., Scarloss, B. A. and Arellano, A. R. (1999). Complex instruction: Equity in cooperative learning classrooms. *Theory into Practice*, 38 (2): 80–86.

Cohen, L. and Manion, L. (1994) *Research Methods in Education*, 4th edn. London: Routledge.

Corbett, J. and Slee, R. (2000) An international conversation on inclusive education. In Armstrong, F., Armstrong, D. and Barton, L. (Eds) *Inclusive Education: Policy, Contexts and Comparative Perspectives*. London: David Fulton.

Creswell, J. W. and Miller, D. L. (2000) Determining validity in qualitative inquiry. *Theory into Practice,* 39 (3): 124–130.

Daniels, D. H. and Perry, K. (2003) 'Learner-centered' according to children. *Theory into Practice*, 42 (2): 102–108.

Davie, R. and Galloway, D. (1996) The voice of the child in education. In Davie, R. and Galloway, D. (Eds), *Listening to Children in Education*. London: David Fulton.

Davies, L. (2000) Researching democratic understanding in primary school. *Research in Education*, 61: 39–48.

Davis, P. (2000) Understanding children's views about reading. PhD thesis. University of Manchester.

Delamont, S. and Hamilton, D. (1993) Revisiting classroom research: A continuing cautionary tale. In Hammersley, M. (Ed.) *Controversies in Classroom Research*, 2nd edn. Buckingham: Open University Press.

Derrington, C. and Kendall, S. (2003) The experiences and perceptions of Gypsy Traveller pupils in English secondary schools. In Shevlin, M. and Rose, R. (Eds) *Encouraging Voices: Respecting the Insights of Young People Who Have Been Marginalised*. Dublin: National Disability Authority.

Dickie-Clark, H. F. (1966) *The Marginal Situation*. London: Routledge and Kegan Paul.

Dockrell, J., Lewis, A. and Lindsay, G. (2000) Researching children's perspectives: A psychological dimension. In Lewis, A. and Lindsay, G. (Eds) *Researching Children's Perspectives*. Buckingham: Open University Press.

Dyson, A., Howes, A. and Roberts, B. (2004) What do we really know about inclusive schools? A systematic review of the research evidence. In Mitchell, D. (Ed.) *Special Educational Needs and Inclusive Education: Major Themes in Education*. London: Routledge.

Elliot, J. (1991) *Action Research for Educational Change*. Buckingham: Open University Press.

Fielding, M. (2001) Students as radical agents of change. *Journal of Educational Change*, 2 (2): 123–141.

Fielding, M. (2004) Transformative approaches to student voice: Theoretical underpinnings, recalcitrant realities. *British Educational Research Journal*, 30 (2): 295–311.

Fine, M. (1991) *Framing Dropouts: Notes on the Politics of an Urban Public High School*. Albany: SUNY Press.

Flekkoy, M. G. and Kaufman, N. H. (1997) *The Participation Rights of the Child: Rights and Responsibilities in Family and Society*. London: Jessica Kingsley.

Florian, L. (1998) Inclusive practice: What, why and how? In Tilstone, C., Florian, L. and Rose, R. (Eds) *Promoting Inclusive Practice*. London: Routledge Falmer.

Fontana, A. and Frey, J. H. (1998) Interviewing: The art of science. In Denzin, N. K. and Lincoln, Y.S. (Eds) *Collecting and Interpreting Qualitative Materials*. London: SAGE.

Fraser, V. (2004) Situating empirical research. In Fraser, V., Lewis, V., Ding, S., Kellett, M. and Robinson, C. (Eds) *Doing Research with Children and Young People*. London: SAGE.

Frederickson, N. and Cline, T. (2009) *Special Educational Needs, Inclusion and Diversity*, 2nd edn. Maidenhead: Open University Press.

Fuchs, L. S., Fuchs, D., Kazdan, S., Karns, K., Calhoon, M. B., Hamlett, C. L. and Hewlett, S. (2000). Effects of workgroup structure and size on student productivity during collaborative work on complex tasks. *Elementary School Journal*, 100 (3): 183–212.

Hall, L. J. and McGregor, J. A. (2000) A follow-up study of the peer relationship of children with disabilities in an inclusive school. *Journal of Special Education*, 34 (3): 114–126.

Harden, J., Scott, S., Backett-Milburn, K. and Jackson, S. (2000) Can't talk, won't talk? Methodological issues in researching children. *Sociological Research Online*, 5 (2). Retrieved 5 October 2000 from http://www.socresonline.org.uk/5/2/harden.html

Hart, R. (1992) *Children's Participation: From Tokenism to Citizenship*. Florence: UNICEF.

Hart, S. (2000) *Thinking through Teaching: A Framework for Enhancing Participation and Learning*. London: David Fulton.

Hart, S., Drummond, M. J. and McIntyre, D. (2007) Learning without limits: Constructing a pedagogy free from determinist beliefs about ability. In Florian, L. (Ed.) *The SAGE Handbook of Special Education*. London: SAGE.

Hazel, N. (1995) Elicitation techniques with young people. *Social Research Update*, 12. Retrieved 16 February 2000 from: http://www.soc.surrey.ac.uk/sru/SRU12.html

Hill, M. (2006) Children's voices on ways of having a voice: Children's and young people's perspectives on methods used in research and consultation. *Childhood*, 13 (1): 69–89.

Hobart, C. and Frankel, J. (2004) *A Practical Guide to Child Observation and Assessment*, 3rd edn. Cheltenham: Nelson Thornes.

Hogan, D. (2005) Researching 'the child' in developmental psychology. In Greene, S. and Hogan, D. (Eds) *Researching Children's Experience: Approaches and Methods*. London: SAGE.

Holt, J. (1964) *How Children Fail*. London: Penguin.

Hopkins, D. (2008) *A Teacher's Guide to Classroom Research*. Maidenhead: Open University Press.

James, A., Jenks, C. and Prout, A. (1998) *Theorizing Childhood*. Cambridge: Polity Press.

Johnson, D., Johnson, R. and Holubec, E. (1993) *Circles of Learning: Cooperation in the Classroom*. Edina, MN: Interaction Books.

Kagan, S. (1992) *Cooperative Learning*. San Clemente, CA: Kagan Cooperative Learning.

Kaplan, I. (2008) Being 'seen' being 'heard': Engaging with students on the margins of education through participatory photography. In Thomson, P. (Ed.) *Doing Visual Research with Children and Young People*. London: Routledge.

Kaplan, I. and Howes, A. (2004) 'Seeing through different eyes': Exploring the value of participative research using images in schools. *Cambridge Journal of Education*, 34 (2): 143–155.

Larkin, P. (1964) *The Whitsun Weddings*. London: Faber & Faber.

Lauchlan, F. and Boyle, C. (2007) Is the use of labels in special education helpful? *Support for Learning*, 22 (1): 36–42.

Lawson, H. (2010) Beyond tokenism? Participation and 'voice' for pupils with significant learning difficulties. In Rose, R. (Ed.) *Confronting Obstacles to Inclusion: International Responses to Developing Inclusive Education*. London: David Fulton.

Lewis, A. (1995) *Children's Understandings of Disability*. London: Routledge.

Lewis, A. (2002) Accessing, through research interviews, the views of children with children difficulties in learning. *Support for Learning*, 17 (3): 110–116.

Lewis, A. (2010) Silence in the context of 'child voice'. *Children and Society*, 24: 14–23.

Lincoln, Y. S. and Guba, E. G. (1985) *Naturalistic Inquiry*. London: SAGE.

Lodge, C. (2005) From hearing voices to engaging in dialogue: Problematising student participation in school improvement. *Journal of Educational Change*, 6: 125–146.

Mahbub, T. (2008) Inclusive education at a BRAC school: Perspectives from the children. *British Journal of Special Education*, 35 (1): 33–41.

Massialas, B. (2001) Hidden curriculum in the classroom. In Smelser, N. J. and Baltes, P. B. (Eds) *International Encyclopedia of the Social and Behavioral Sciences*. Oxford: Elsevier.

Mauthner, M. (1997) Methodological aspects of collecting data from children: Lessons from three research projects. *Children and Society*, 11 (1): 16–28.

Maxwell, J.A. (1992) Understanding and validity in qualitative research. *Harvard Educational Review*, 62 (3): 279–300.

Mayall, B. (2001) Conversations with children: Working with generational issues. In Christensen, P. and James, A. (Eds) *Research with Children: Perspectives and Practices*. London: RoutledgeFalmer.

McIntyre, D. and Macleod, G. (1993) The characteristics and uses of systematic classroom observation. In Hammersley, M. (Ed.) *Controversies in Classroom Research*, 2nd edn. Buckingham: Open University Press.

McKernan, J. (1996) *Curriculum Action Research*, 2nd edn. London: Kogan Page.

McNamara, S. and Moreton, G. (1995) *Changing Behaviour: Teaching Children with Emotional and Behavioural Difficulties in Primary and Secondary Classrooms*. London: David Fulton.

McNiff, J. and Whitehead, J. (2010) *You and Your Action Research Project*, 3rd edn. London: Routledge.

Messiou, K. (2002) Marginalisation in primary schools: Listening to children's voices. *Support for Learning*, 17 (3): 117–121.

Messiou, K. (2003) Conversations with children: A pathway towards understanding marginalisation and inclusive education. PhD thesis. University of Manchester.

Messiou, K. (2006a) Conversations with children: Making sense of marginalisation in primary school settings. *European Journal of Special Needs Education*, 21 (1): 39–54.

Messiou, K. (2006b) Understanding marginalisation in education: The voice of children. *European Journal of Psychology of Education*, 21 (3) (special issue): 305–318.

Messiou, K. (2008a) Encouraging children to think in more inclusive ways. *British Journal of Special Needs Education*, 35 (1): 26–32.

Messiou, K. (2008b) Understanding children's constructions of meanings about other children: Implications for inclusive education. *Journal of Research in Special Educational Needs*, 8 (1): 26–32.

Messiou, K. (2011) Collaborating with children in exploring marginalisation: ·An approach to inclusive education. *International Journal of Inclusive Education*. DOI: 10.1080/13603116.2011.572188

Messiou, K. (in preparation) Exploring barriers to learning and participation of potentially vulnerable groups of students in higher education.

Messiou, K. and Jones, L. (2011) Using students' voices as a strategy for addressing challenges in urban schools. Paper presented at ECER (European Conference of Educational Research), Berlin.

Miles, M. B. and Huberman, A. M. (1994) *Qualitative Data Analysis*. London: SAGE.

Miles, S. and Ainscow, M. (2011) *Responding to Diversity in Schools: An Inquiry Based Approach*. London: Routledge.

Miller, J. and Glassner, B. (1997) The 'inside' and the 'outside': Finding realities in interviews. In Silverman, D. (Ed.) *Qualitative Research: Theory, Method and Practice*. London: SAGE.

Mills, J. and Mills, R. (2000) Introduction. In Mills, J. and Mills, R. (Eds) *Childhood Studies: A Reader in Perspectives of Childhood*. London: Routledge.

Mills, R. (2000) Perspectives of childhood. In Mills, J. and Mills, R. (Eds) *Childhood Studies: A Reader in Perspectives of Childhood*. London: Routledge.

Mitra, D. L. (2003) Student voice in school reform: Reframing student–teacher relationships. *McGill Journal of Education*, 38 (2): 289–304.

Mitra, D. L. (2004) The significance of students: Can increasing 'student voice' in schools lead to gains in youth development? *Teachers College Record*, 106 (4): 651–688.

Mittler, P. (2000) *Working towards Inclusive Education: Social Contexts*. London: David Fulton.

Mordal, K. N. and Stromstad, M. (1998) Norway: Adapted education for all? In Booth, T. and Ainscow, M. (Eds) *From Them to Us*. London: Routledge.

Moreno, J. L. (1934) *Who Shall Survive?* New York: Beacon House.

Morrow, V. and Richards, M. (1996) The ethics of social research with children: An overview. *Children and Society*, 10 (2): 90–105.

Nikolaraizi, M. and Reybekiel, N. D. (2001) A comparative study of children's attitudes towards deaf children, children in wheelchairs and blind children in Greece and in the UK. *European Journal of Special Needs Education*, 16 (2): 167–182.

O'Kane, C. (2000) The development of participatory techniques: Facilitating children's views about decisions which affect them. In Christensen, P. and James, A. (Eds) *Research with Children: Perspectives and Practices*. London: RoutledgeFalmer.

Pierson, J. (2001) *Tackling Social Exclusion*. London: Routledge.

Pilcher, J. and Wagg, S. (1996) Introduction: Thatcher's children? In Pilcher, J. and Wagg, S. (Eds) *Thatcher's Children? Politics, Childhood and Society in the 1980s and 1990s*. London: Falmer Press.

Pollard, A. (1985) *The Social World of the Primary School*. London: Holt, Rinehart and Winston.

Pollard, A. (1996) *The Social World of Children's Learning*. London: Cassell.

Prout, A. (2002) Researching children as social actors: An introduction to the children 5–16 programme. *Children and Society*, 16 (2): 67–76.

Prout, A. and James, A. (1990) Introduction. In James, A. and Prout, A. (Eds) *Constructing and Reconstructing Childhood: Contemporary Issues in the Sociological Study of Childhood*. London: Falmer Press.

Punch, S. (2002a) Interviewing strategies with young people: The 'secret box' stimulus material and task-based activities. *Children and Society*, 16 (1): 45–56.

Punch, S. (2002b) Research with children: The same or different from research with adults? *Childhood*, 9 (3): 321–341.

Quicke, J. (2003) Educating the pupil voice. *Support for Learning*, 18 (2), 51–57.

Qvortrup, J. (1994) Childhood matters: An introduction. In Qvortrup, J., Bardy, M., Sgritta, G. and Wintersberger, H. (Eds) *Childhood Matters: Social Theory, Practice and Politics*. Aldershot: Avebury.

Raymond, L. (2001) Student involvement in school improvement: From data source to significant voice. *Forum*, 43 (2): 58–61.

Richardson, L. (1998) Writing: A method of inquiry. In Denzin, N. K. and Lincoln, Y. S. (Eds) *Collecting and Interpreting Qualitative Materials*. London: SAGE.

Riddall-Leech, S. (2005) *How to Observe Children*. Oxford: Heinemann.

Rieser, R. (2011) Disability, human rights and inclusive education, and why inclusive education is the only educational philosophy and practice that makes sense in today's world. In Richards, G. and Armstrong, F. (Eds) *Teaching and Learning in Diverse and Inclusive Classrooms*. London: Routledge.

Roaf, C. (2002) Editorial: Children and young people: Advocacy and empowerment. *Support for Learning*, 17 (3): 102–103.

Roberts, H. (2000) Listening to children: And hearing them. In Christensen, P. and James, A. (Eds) *Research with Children: Perspectives and Practices*. London: RoutledgeFalmer.

Robson, C. (1993) *Real World Research*. Oxford: Blackwell.

Rowland, S. (1984) *The Enquiring Classroom*. Lewes: Falmer Press.

Rudduck, J. and Flutter, J. (2000) Pupil participation and pupil perspective: 'Carving a new order of experience'. *Cambridge Journal of Education*, 30 (1): 75–89.

Sammons, P. (1989) Ethical issues and statistical work. In Burgess, R. G. (Ed.) *The Ethics of Educational Research*. London: Falmer Press.

Sapon-Shevin, M. (1990) Student support through cooperative learning. In Stainback, W. and Stainback, S. (Eds) *Support Networks for Inclusive Schooling*. Baltimore: PaulHBrookes.

Sebba, J. and Ainscow, M. (1996) International developments in inclusive schooling: Mapping the issues. *Cambridge Journal of Education*, 26 (1): 5–18.

Schon, D. A. (1987) *Educating the Reflective Practitioner*. San Francisco: Jossey-Bass Publishers.

Sharman, C., Cross, W. and Vennis, D. (2003) *Observing Children*, 3rd edn. London: Continuum.

Silva, E. (2001) 'Squeaky wheels and flat tires': A case study of students as reform participants. *Forum*, 43(2): 95–99.

Silverman, D. (2001) *Interpreting Qualitative Data*, 2nd edn. London: SAGE.

Skrtic, T. M. (1986) The crisis in special education knowledge: A perspective on perspectives. *Focus on Exceptional Children*, 18 (7): 1–16.

Smidt, S. (2005) *Observing, Assessing and Planning for Children in the Early Years*. London: RoutledgeFalmer.

Strauss, A. and Corbin, J. (1990) *Basics of Qualitative Research: Grounded Theory Procedures and Techniques*. London: SAGE.

Sugerman, D. (1991) *The Doors: The Complete Illustrated Lyrics*. London: MacDonald and Co.

Tangen, R. (2009) Conceptualising quality of school life from pupils' perspectives: A four dimensional model. *International Journal of Inclusive Education*, 13 (8): 829–844.

Thomas, N. and O'Kane, C. (1998) The ethics of participatory research with children. *Children and Society*, 12 (5): 336–348.

Thomson, P. (2008a) Children and young people: Voices in visual research. In Thomson, P. (Ed.) *Doing Visual Research with Children and Young People*. London: Routledge.

Thomson, P. (Ed.) (2008b) *Doing Visual Research with Children and Young People*. London: Routledge.

Thomson, P. (2010) Involving children and young people in educational change: Possibilities and challenges. In Hargreaves, A., Lieberman, A., Fullan, M. and Hopkins, D. (Eds) *Second International Handbook of Educational Change*. London: Springer.

UIS (UNESCO Institute for Statistics) (2011) *Out of School Children: New Data Reveal New Challenges*. Fact Sheet, June 2011, No. 12. UNESCO: Quebec.

UNDP (1996) *Georgia Human Development Report 1996: Glossary*. Retrieved 20 October 2008, from http://www.undp.org/rbec/nhdr/1996/georgia/glossary.htm

UNESCO (United Nations Educational, Scientific and Cultural Organisation) (2010) *EFA Global Monitoring Report: Reaching the Marginalized*. Paris: UNESCO.

United Nations (1989) *The UN Convention on the Rights of the Child*. New York: UN. Also available at http://www.unicef.org/crc/crc.htm

Veck, W. (2009) Listening to include. *International Journal of Inclusive Education*, 13 (2): 141–155.

Vlachou, A. D. (1997) *Struggles for Inclusive Education*. Buckingham: Open University Press.

Walker, R. and Adelman, C. (1993) Interaction analysis in informal classrooms: A critical comment on the Flander's system. In Hammersley, M. (Ed.) *Controversies in Classroom Research*, 2nd edn. Buckingham: Open University Press.

Wang, C. C., Yi, W. K., Tao, Z. W. and Carovano, K. (1998) Photovoice as a participatory health promotion strategy. *Health Promotion International*, 13 (1): 75–86.

Wasserman, S. and Faust, K. (1994) *Social Network Analysis: Methods and Applications*. Cambridge: Cambridge University Press.

Watts, M. and Ebbutt, D. (1987) More than the sum of the parts: Research methods in group interviewing. *British Educational Research Journal*, 13 (1): 25–34.

Wragg, E. C. (2000) *An Introduction to Classroom Observation*, 2nd edn. London: RoutledgeFalmer.

Wyse, D. (2001) Felt tip pens and school councils: Children's participation rights in four English schools. *Children and Society*, 15 (4): 209–218.

Index